Design:Portfolio

To Virginia, Nancy, and Anna.

© 2013 Rockport Publishers

First published in the United States of America in 2013
by Rockport Publishers, a member of
Quarto Publishing Group USA Inc.
100 Cummings Center
Suite 406-L
Beverly, Massachusetts 01915-6101
Telephone: (978) 282-9590
Fax: (978) 283-2742
www.rockpub.com
Visit RockPaperInk.com to share your opinions, creations, and passion for design.

10 9 8 7 6 5 4 3 2

ISBN: 978-1-59253-840-9

Digital edition published in 2013
eISBN: 978-1-61058-785-3

Library of Congress Cataloging-in-Publication Data

Design portfolios (Rockport Publishers)
     Design Portfolio: Self-promotion at its best
     Summary: "Featuring a curated collection of approximately 300 exquisite designs, along with essays from designers in the field about the essence and importance of a good portfolio design, Design: Portfolio contains mini-workshops that dissect several featured projects and highlight the effectiveness of exceptional design treatments from around the world. Designers will discover the underlying details that make each design so special. This is an exciting new addition to the informative and inspiring Design series by Rockport Publishers that offers the best of design in practice"-- Provided by publisher.
ISBN 978-1-59253-840-9 (pbk.)
1. Art portfolios. 2. Commercial art--Themes, motives. 3. Design services--Marketing. I. Go Welsh (Firm) II. Title.
NC1001.D47 2013
741.6--dc23

                                                          2012039093

Design: Go Welsh

Printed in China

Design: Portfolio

Self-promotion at its best

Rockport Publishers
100 Cummings Center, Suite 406L
Beverly, MA 01915

rockpub.com • rockpaperink.com

Craig Welsh/
Go Welsh

Foreword

Three months of gathering design portfolios and self-promotions resulted in a collection of more than 1,800 images. *Design: Portfolio* features more than 300 outstanding portfolio and self-promotions from exceptional designers and studios around the world.

The range of projects submitted and featured in the book is as varied as the designers and studios producing the work—books, brochures, buttons, packaging, postcards, wearables, and much more. Twenty Closer Look features in the book offer brief commentary on specific design details that are worthy of closer inspection.

We also asked five highly respected designers to talk about what makes a great portfolio and self-promotion. Each essay was written specifically for this volume by some of the most experienced and creatively successful design professionals as well as some who are still in the earlier stages of their careers and quickly making names for themselves.

Three cheers for design!

Design:
Portfolio

SELF-PROMOTION AT ITS BEST

CRAIG WELSH

Introduction

Admittedly, the notion of "portfolio" has shifted dramatically in a very brief period of time.

Portfolio as object, a case that houses physical samples of work, has seemingly been replaced by portfolio as content, an ever-malleable set of digital samples of work that can morph and adapt at a moment's notice to all manner of media.

The making of a design portfolio had typically been a very laborious task that involved tedious, time-consuming, and often expensive reproduction methods. Crafting a collection of one's design work required adept use of craft knives and metal straightedges, and a well-ventilated area in which to use spray adhesive. However, as less expensive, short-run, digital printing has gained increasing acceptance and PDF files, websites, blogs, and social media have provided near-immediate updating of a designer's most recent work, the time and monetary investments in showcasing one's work have shifted.

Nonetheless, as evidenced by this book's content, the most critical elements in creating successful and memorable design portfolios and self-promotions still hold true, regardless of the media employed: Thoughtful creativity and an unrelenting commitment to details are the core elements of design that arrest attention and compel action.

At a time when designers are more often thinking of personal branding and their individuality, it's reassuring to see a book, such as this one, take its place in the world. It reminds us that designers are part of a larger community and that there is lasting value in the physical presence of design.

This book is a volume of shared pages, ideas, and methods by which to teach, learn, and be inspired. The design community's portfolio is in your hands. Enjoy.

NICK ASBURY
Bollington, Cheshire, United Kingdom

Show Off

Woody Allen said that 90% of success is showing up. Looking at the design industry, you could say the other 10% is showing off. Self-initiated and self-promotional work has always played a big part, both for rising stars making their names and global firms keen on maintaining a creative reputation.

There's nothing wrong with this. Indeed, there's a lot right with it. Simply moving from one client brief to another is a passive existence for any creative person. A self-initiated project is a chance to explore ideas and elements of your craft that would otherwise never see the light of day.

There's a subtle distinction between self-promotional work and self-initiated work. The former is explicitly produced for the purpose of promoting yourself—that's the only reason it exists. It might be a book detailing your best projects or a mailer talking about your company approach.

Self-initiated projects are different. They're ideas you pursue yourself, without the involvement of a client, but that have a purpose beyond self-promotion. For me, this is an interesting seam to explore. It might be a book of poetry rearranging the words on corporate websites or inventing the language equivalent of the Pantone® color-matching system. If you pursue an idea you find interesting, there's a good chance other people will too.

Of course, self-promotion is a useful side effect when these projects go well. But the same is true of client work. Do a great job for a client and it won't just be good for them. Your firm's reputation grows by association, among your peer group and other potential clients. In that sense, all work is self-promotional. You just have to make sure the world knows about it—which brings us back to showing off.

However you do it, showing off has to be done. Many of the best things that happen in any creative career come about through serendipity: striking up a friendship with a like-minded collaborator, or bumping into the right client at the right time. Showing off helps serendipity happen. The more visible you are to your peers and the world at large, the more likely it is you'll get that magical, career-changing email out of the blue. That's partly why I said yes to writing this article—it's a form of showing off. And you never know who might be reading.

Yurko
Gutsulyak

"Daring" comment in copy is an
accurate reflection of the overall
mood of the piece.

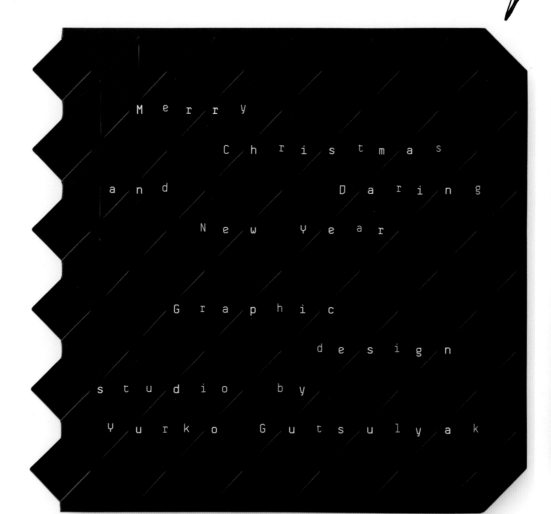

Merry
Christmas
and   Daring
New   Year

Graphic
design
studio   by
Yurko   Gutsulyak

www.gstu o.com.ua

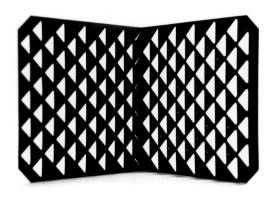

See-through sexy

Very tight registration with printing, diecutting, and finishing. Fascinating attention to detail.

FIRM
Graphic Design
Studio by Yurko
Gutsulyak

PROJECT
Dragon Card

ART DIRECTOR
Yurko Gutsulyak

DESIGNER
Yurko Gutsulyak

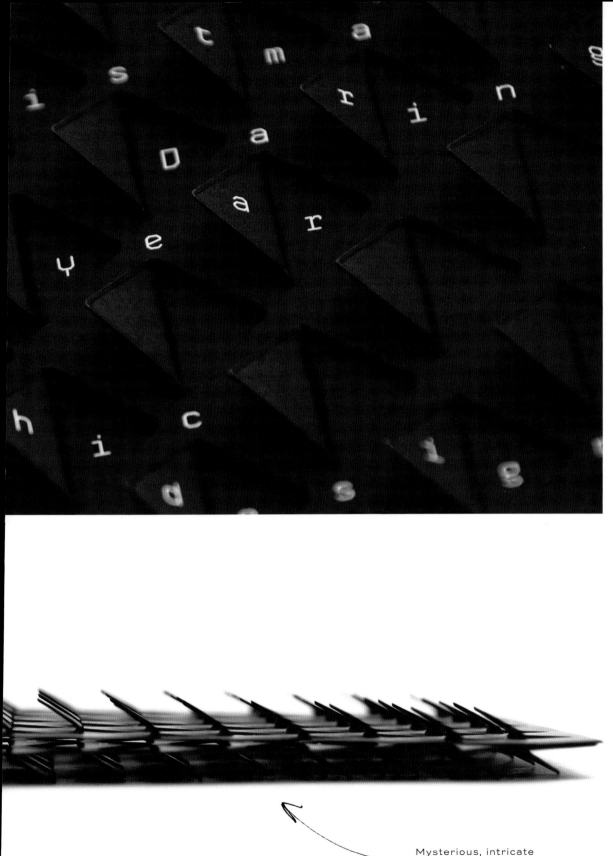

Mysterious, intricate
diecuts and folds

FIRM
hat-trick

PROJECT
In Brief Book

ART DIRECTORS
Jim Sutherland
Gareth Howat

DESIGNER
Alexander Jurua

FIRM
Elfen 10

PROJECT
Self-Promotion
Brochure & Poster

017

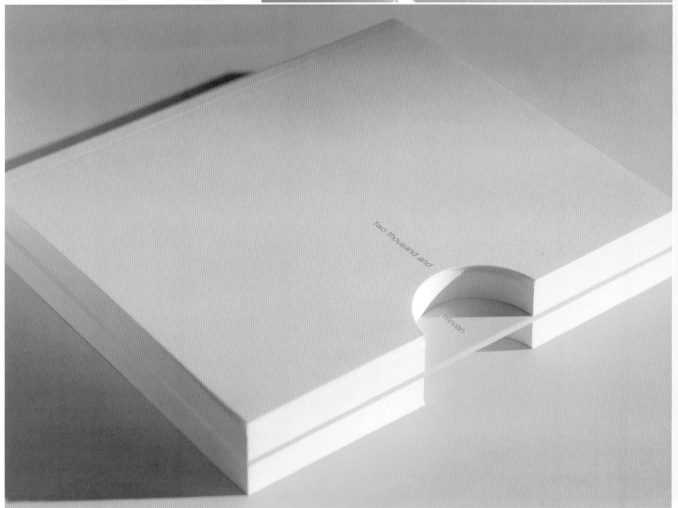

FIRM	PROJECT	ART DIRECTOR	DESIGNER
Matter Strategic Design	Matter 2011 Notebook	Mike Kasperski	Mike Kasperski

FIRM
Exit 10 Advertising

PROJECT
Exit 10
Christmas Card

ART DIRECTOR
Carl Nielson

DESIGNER
Carl Nielson

FIRM
Base Art Co.

PROJECT
Self-Promotion
Mailers

ART DIRECTOR
Terry Rohrbach

DESIGNERS
Terry Rohrbach
Drue Dixon

020   Design: Portfolio

HOT.

ot Yum Yum?

Sakura Japanese Steakhouse came to us with a goal
of launching their restaurant in a very upscale area or
Easton Town Center, one of the country's premiere
retail destinations. (On the off chance you don't
speak Japanese, Sakura means cherry blossom.) So
leveraging that influence along with the rich visuals of
Japanese culture, we helped create this brand from
scratch designing their identity, menus, lobby cards,
exterior signage and a micro site.

SAKURA

BASE
ART CO.

MANTRA No. 05

Design is art at work.

At Base Art Co., we uphold certain truths that guide us and fuel our
passion to create great design communications that inspire, motivate,
and differentiate. Design is art at work...honestly.

In working with Sakura Japanese Restaurant, our mission was to create
a memorable environment that brought the brand to life through
multiple customer touch points. Take a look at our case study or check
out our Web site, baseartco.com, for more on Sakura.

We'd love the opportunity to get together to learn more about your
company and share a few case studies that are relevant to the types of
services you provide. Call us or we'll call you; either way let's chat.

Best,

Terry Rohrbach
Principal

17 BRICKEL ST. STE D. COLUMBUS, OH 43215, 614.224.4535 BASEARTCO.COM

BASE ART CO.

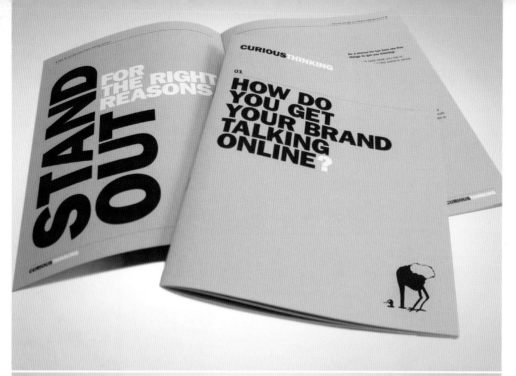

FIRM	PROJECT	ART DIRECTOR	DESIGNER
Curious	Curious Thinking Mailer	Curious	Curious

FIRM	PROJECT	ART DIRECTORS	DESIGNERS
Hybrid Design	*Work & Play*	Dora Drimalas	Ed O'Brien
		Brian Flynn	Caleb Kozlowski

FIRM	PROJECT	ART DIRECTOR	DESIGNER
5Seven	5Seven	Clint Delapaz	Clint Delapaz
	Self-Promotion		

FIRM
Studio Usher

PROJECT
Make Your Mark
Booklet

ART DIRECTOR
Naomi Usher

DESIGNER
Naomi Usher

FIRM
C&G Partners

PROJECT
Brand Identities
Book

ART DIRECTORS
Emanuela Frigerio
Steff Geissbuhler

DESIGNER
Hyun Auh

FIRM
Ross Chandler
Creative

PROJECT
Portfolio Handout

ART DIRECTOR
Ross Chandler

DESIGNER
Ross Chandler

GANG
MORE THAN JUST THAT
GROUP OF MIDDLE-SCHOOLERS
WHO JUMPED YOU FOR YOUR
MILK MONEY

PMS
MORE THAN JUST
THAT BEAST YOU OFFER
SACRIFICIAL
CHOCOLATE
TO ONCE A MONTH

PROOF
MORE THAN JUST THE REASON
YOU WENT ON A
DAYTIME TALK SHOW
TO FIND OUT WHO'S YOUR
BABY DADDY

SCORE
MORE THAN JUST
GETTING THAT
TALL DRINK OF WATER
OUT OF THE BAR
& INTO YOUR BED

RESOLUTION
MORE THAN JUST THAT VO
TO HIT THE GYM DAILY A
STOP SNACK
WHILE SITTING AT YO

DIE
MORE THAN JUST THAT PREDICTABLE
THING THAT HAPPENS TO
ERY HOT CHICK
OR FILMS

FIRM	PROJECT	ART DIRECTOR	DESIGNER
Gilah Press & Design	Designerds Postcards	Kat Feuerstein	Katie Smith

CLOSER LOOK

Justin Speers

Minimal color palette
allows work to be
center of attention.

Self-mailer design
saves time and money.

JUSTIN
SPEERS
· 1121 Grove Rd ·
WEST CHESTER, PA
1 9 3 8 0

Hand-cut
masking tape
serves as
closure.

PACKAGE AS A WEBSITE

A project to take a six-sided box and
transcribe all the textual informaton into an
abstracted six-page site including a homepage.

Everyday materials like
reinforced packaging
tape and stock
envelopes from office
supply store

FIRM
Justin Speers

PROJECT
Portfolio
Mailer

ART DIRECTOR
Justin Speers

DESIGNER
Justin Speers

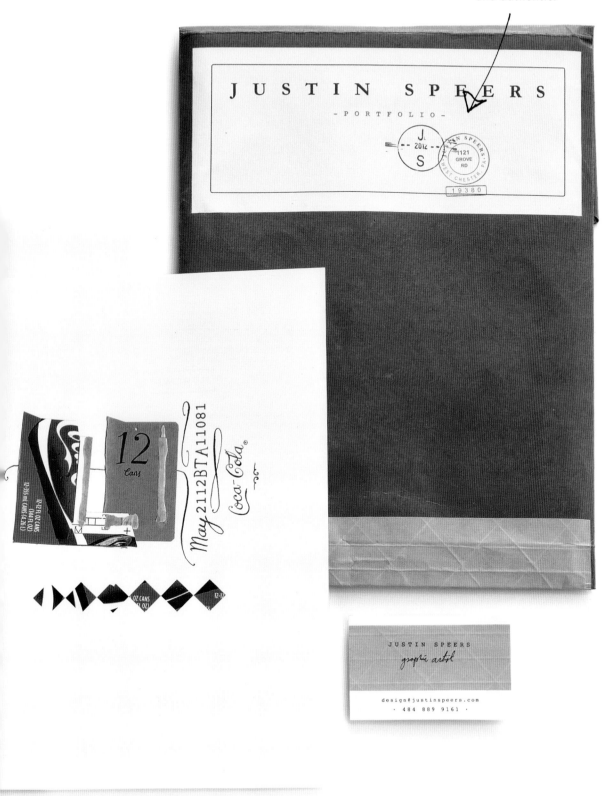

Postal stamp design crafts a sense of the piece being official and authentic.

FIRM
Chris Maghintay

PROJECT
Self-Promotion
Materials

DESIGNER
Chris Maghintay

FIRM	**PROJECT**	**ART DIRECTOR**	**DESIGNER**
MDG, Inc.	Agency Promo Book	Tim Merry	Kris Greene

FIRM	PROJECT	ART DIRECTOR	DESIGNER
Funnel: Eric Kass	*Funnel: The Fine Commercial Art Practice of Eric Kass*	Eric Kass	Eric Kass

FIRM	PROJECT	ART DIRECTOR	DESIGNER
9 Myles, Inc	Self-Promotion	Myles McGuiness	Myles McGuiness

FIRM	PROJECT	ART DIRECTORS	DESIGNER
Ologie	Ologie Capabilities Book	Bev Bethge Kelly Ruoff	Dan McMahon

FIRM
Studio Usher

PROJECT
Postcard: Sunny
Summer Solstice

ART DIRECTOR
Naomi Usher

DESIGNER
Naomi Usher

FIRM
Smbolic

PROJECT
SM Self-Promo

ART DIRECTORS
Kevin Krueger
Dave Mason
Greg Samata

DESIGNER
Kevin Krueger

FIRM
Alt Group

PROJECT
This Over That

ART DIRECTOR
Dean Poole

DESIGNERS
Dean Poole
Tony Proffit

041

Design
Ranch

One-color printing on
textured cloth
creates a tactile
experience.

Pop-up promotion
within the promotion
provides an unexpected
and fun divergence.

Slipcase housing for the promotion elevates the specialness of the piece to that of opening a gift.

FIRM
Design Ranch

PROJECT
Design Ranch
Big Books

ART DIRECTORS
Ingred Sidie
Michelle Sonderegger

Dramatic scale shift
provides a memorably
big impact.

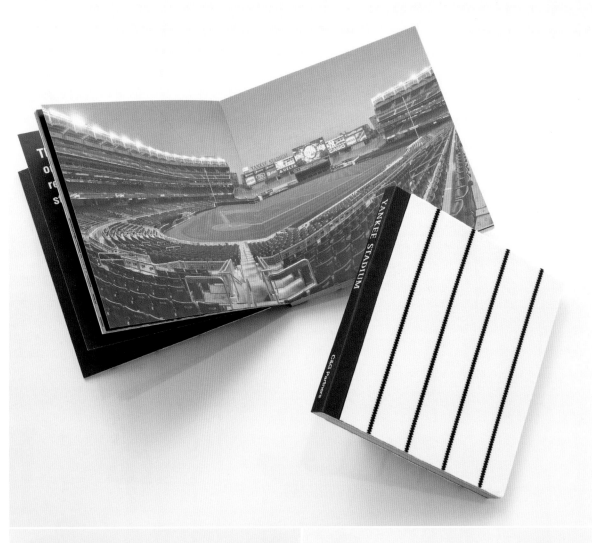

FIRM
C&G Partners

PROJECT
Yankees
Monograph

ART DIRECTOR
Emanuela Frigerio

DESIGNERS
Craig Gephart
Keith Helmetag

FENWAY PARK 2002—2012
ASHTON DESIGN

10/100

FIRM
Ashton Design

PROJECT
Ashton Design:
10/100 Book

ART DIRECTOR
Ronnie Yountz

DESIGNER
Jennie Romei
Hoffman

FIRM
FK Design

PROJECT
Presentazione FK

ART DIRECTOR
Federico Frasson

DESIGNER
Federico Frasson

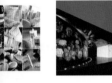 

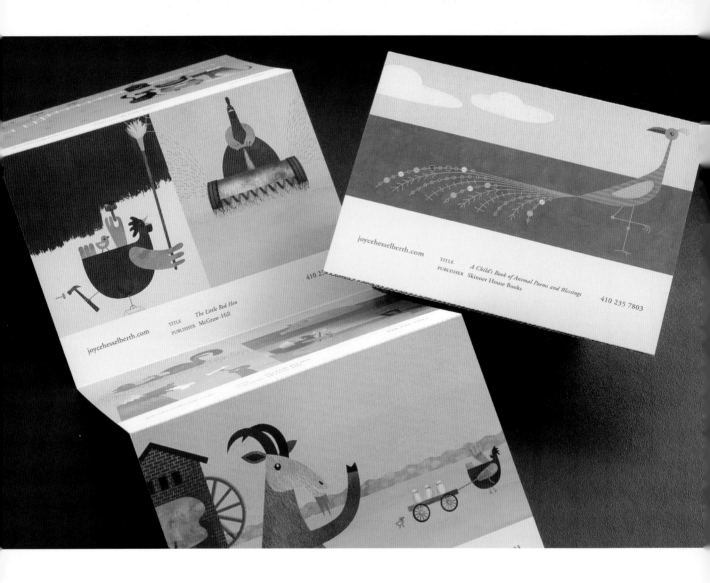

TITLE The Little Red Hen
PUBLISHER McGraw-Hill

joycehesselberth.com

joycehesselberth.com

TITLE A Child's Book of Animal Poems and Blessings
PUBLISHER Skinner House Books

410 235 7803

FIRM
Spur Design

PROJECT
Illustration
Promo 2011

ART DIRECTOR
Joyce Hesselberth

DESIGNER
Joyce Hesselberth

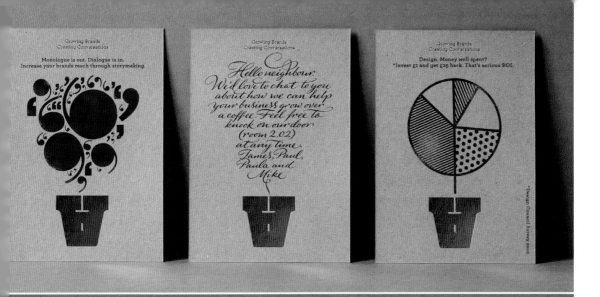

FIRM
The Allotment

PROJECT
Seed Packet
Business Card
and Mailer

ART DIRECTORS
James Backhurst
Michael Smith
Paula Talford

DESIGNER
James Backhurst

FIRM
Studio Usher

PROJECT
Postcard:
Supersize
Your Brand

ART DIRECTOR
Naomi Usher

DESIGNER
Naomi Usher

Silly Willie.

For your next design project
BASE ART CO.

www.baseartco.com

A NEW TRANSLATION
BASE ART CO.

FIRM
Base Art Co.

PROJECT
Base Art Co.
Postcards

ART DIRECTOR
Terry Rohrbach

DESIGNER
Terry Rohrbach

CLOSER LOOK

Alex
Trochut

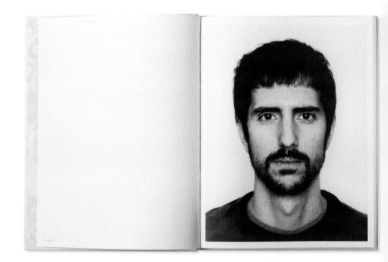

Embossed cover
pattern provides
degree of care and
importance to the
piece with minimal
typographic
intrusion.

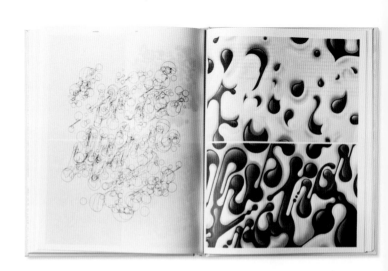

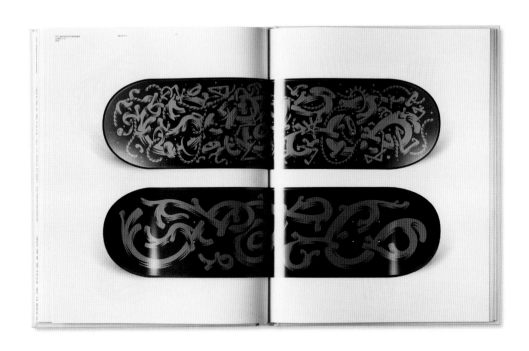

Front and back
covers printed with
glow-in-the-dark ink

More Is More title and
cover aesthetic are
ironically minimal.

XFUNS

XFuns, a Taiw
for a cover an
commission w
graphic device
Nouveau, with
kind used wide
The underlyin
limit, to the po
design also ho
baroque and n
a factor in visu

FIRM
Alex Trochut

PROJECT
More Is More
Book

ART DIRECTOR
Alex Trochut

DESIGNER
Alex Trochut

Sketches provide backstory to process by which design is achieved.

ne, asked Alex
of its issues. The
Alex taking as his
f typical of Art
ble forms of the
n of the period.
gibility to the
abstraction. The
ween overwrought
he is made to be

With this Art Nouveau decorative technique, and using a typographic base, he designed the words Type (for the cover) and Soul (for the back cover). The use of colour and of the subsequent light and shade gives a great sense of rhythm to the final composition. The design included incorporating the magazine's brand, achieved with an elegant logo in black and white.

See this project at page 80

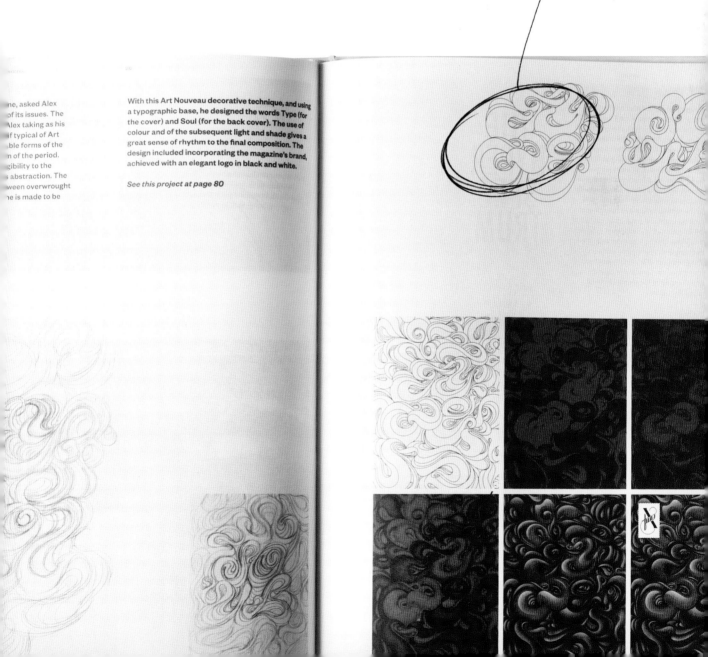

FIRM
Hucklebuck Design

PROJECT
Hucklebuck
"Living"
Postcard Mailer

ART DIRECTOR
Andy Hayes

DESIGNER
Andy Hayes

FIRM
Spunk Design
Machine

PROJECT
Sweet Life Promo

ART DIRECTOR
Jeff Johnson

DESIGNER
Lucas Richards

FIRM
10 Associates

PROJECT
10 Things You
Should Know
About Branding

ART DIRECTOR
Jill Peel

DESIGNER
Michael Freemantle

FIRM
id29

PROJECT
Slay the
Scary Monsters
Campaign

ART DIRECTOR
Doug Bartow

DESIGNER
Doug Bartow

CLOSER LOOK

AvroKO

Color palette
consistent
throughout
entire space

Mix of architecture, interior design, and graphic design; branded experience

AQUATIC
DELIGHTS

EAST OR WEST COAST
OYSTERS
See punch card for selection.

Shrimp cocktail, Sriracha
cocktail sauce $4/piece

Grilled & chilled octopus salad,
shaved fennel, smoked almonds $12

Razor clam & egg salad,
toasted baguette $10
Add ½ ounce of American hackleback
caviar $50

{ THE SEAFOOD
TOWER }
MINI $20
MEDIUM $67
LARGE $125

A FINE PAIRING
CHAMPAGNE &
A SELECTION FROM
THE SEA

ENJOY A SEAFOOD TOWER
WITH A GLASS
OF DOM PERIGNON $49

charcuterie

Country pork pâté, pistachios,
dates $10

Rabbit & foie gras terrine $14

A BIT OF
EVERYTHING
THE PLATE

Daily selection of cured meats &
cheese plate, olives, pickles $20

cheese

azy Lady
ws' milk.

T)

Crème caramel, rum raisins,
grilled pineapple, coconut foam
$9

Chocolate soufflé, PAROLE
hiskey ice cream (Please allow
inutes) $9

namon sugar doughnuts,
chocolate sauce $9

Cauliflower & gruyère gratin $7

Whole grain mustard mashed
potatoes $6

French fries, chili ket
cheese mayo $6

Wheat berry salad,
cucumber, Marcona

side

A PREVIEW OF W

desse

BOOZY
ICE CREAM
All three for $9

PAROLE Whiskey
Bourbon Butter Pecan
Strawberry Fig & Port

Hand-cut salmon tartare, fried
capers, roasted peppers, soft-
boiled quail egg $12

Shaved roasted beets, watercress,
sweet spiced pecans, Paisley
Farms feta cheese $10

Foie gras & five spice terrine,
grilled peach & red onion relish
$17

Prince Edward Island mussels, fire
roasted piquillo peppers, tomato,
caper broth $13

LAND

Grilled Berkshire pork chop,
purple potato salad, quince
& apple sauce $26

Guinness & five spice glazed
short rib (for two) $44

Summer pea ravioli, vine tomato,
arugula & Parmesan $20

Roasted organic half chicken,
charred fennel, Kalamata olives,
orange, sun dried tomatoes $24

Cheesecake, nectarine compote
lemon sorbet $9

Carrot cake, fried carrots, almond
ice cream $9

Mother-in-law's Christmas
pudding, grilled plums, hard sauce
ice cream $9

second c

S+P STE

CERTIFIED BLACK
FROM CREEKSTONE F
DRY AGED FOR 28 DAYS
BONE-MARROW BEAR
MADE STEAK

Fillet (7oz)

NY Strip steak (7o
Ribeye for two (28

THE BUR

S+P dry aged An
with Pennsylvan
maple bacon & a f

NU FOR THE EVENING

first cour

HOUSEMADE
RE SURE TO
TRY OUR
SEASONAL POTS OF DE
SERVED WITH GRILLED
BREAD, BEST SHARED.

Portabello mus
mousse, PAROLE
& truffle jell

Chicken liver mou
pepper jelly

316 BOWERY AT BLEECKER ST.

FRO

Cockta

W. L. Weller 12 year, carpano antica vermout
Manhattan 'On Dra

Brooklyn gin, house made tonic, grapefruit
Gin & Tonic

Plymouth gin, dolin dry vermouth, accoutrement
Dry Martini Service

Bols genever, kirschwasser, lemon, cranberry marmalade
New Amsterdam

Bombay sapphire 'east', applejack, lemon, house made grenadine, egg wh
Pink Lady

Cognac, rye, green chartreuse, st. germain, absinthe, peychaud's bitters $14
Pecan & Maple Sazerac

Spring 44 gin, green chartreuse, st. germain, fresh celery, verjus $14
Celery Gimlet

Compass box, mezcal, fillet blanc, drambuie, lemon bitters, oak $16
Prince Edward Cocktail 'Barrel Aged'

Espolon blanco, mezcal, yellow chartreuse, fresh bell pepper, chili oil $14
Bowery Fix

Fat washed rhum agricole, lime, pink peppercorn $14
Cracked Pepper Daiquiri

Leblon cachaca, poire william, fall spices, hard apple cider $14
Lower East Cider

Corralejo reposado, mezcal, fresh beet, vanilla, ginger $14
Beetnik

Campari, combier triple sec, blood orange, sparkling rosé, rose water $13
Sanguine

Barsol pisco, spiced pineapple, lime $14
Pisco Punch

+ PAROLE
QUATIC DELIGHTS

Menu design is highly organized
with use of rules to define space.

Horses are consistent
elements from
business cards to
menus to interior art.

316 BOWERY
NEW YORK, NY 10012

WWW.SAXONANDPAROLE.COM

212.254.0350

SAXON + PAROLE

SANGUINE

OWER EAST CIDE

A POIRE WILLIAM SPICES

CELERY GIMI

ST GERMAIN, GREEN CHART

BEETN

FIRM	PROJECT	ART DIRECTORS
AvroKO	Restaurant Identity/Interiors: Saxon + Parole	Kristina O'Neal Greg Bradshaw Adam Farmerie William Harris

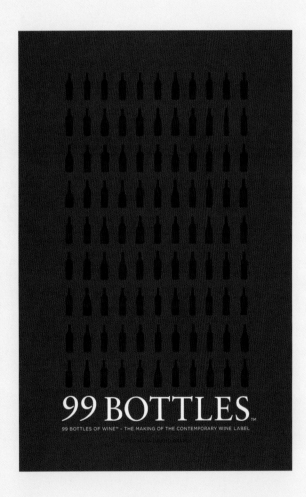

FIRM
CF Napa

PROJECT
*99 Bottles of
Wine* Book

ART DIRECTOR
David Schuemann

DESIGNER
Dana Deininger

Slingshot

COMPANY SLINGSHOT WINES
APPELATION NAPA VALLEY, CALIFORNIA

In 1999, a Houston-based businessman named Michael Stewart sold his computer business and came to the Napa Valley with the dream of making great wine. To get his new Stewart Cellars off on the right foot, he hired the celebrated consulting winemaker Paul Hobbs to create a super-premium Napa Valley Cabernet Sauvignon. It was a brilliant start, and six years later Michael's son James left a budding career in reality TV in Los Angeles and came to the Napa Valley to help his father and learn the wine business from the ground up. Out on the road selling wine, young James spotted an opportunity: use unsold grapes from his dad's vineyard to make a line of lower-priced wines aimed at younger consumers. That idea gave birth to Slingshot.

His marketing pitch is a bulls eye, "Slingshot," James says, "is about putting your best foot forward while forgetting about fitting into the mold or following the rules. Be bold, be adventurous, choose your own path, and above all remember to have fun."

Its in this spirit Slingshot wines approached CF Napa to revitalize and refocus their brand back to its core values and brand essence. Their label did not match their young and irreverent message — a total disconnect between their brand story and the reality of the packaging. CF Napa decided to explore other icons to support the slingshot icon. The bulls-eye was perfect, both familiar and clean, and on concept.

The ultimate solution places the vintage date on the target making it feel as if it has been shot at already. The shot's resulting hole is diecut through the label so that the glass of the bottle shows through. Highly technical to achieve, collaboration with a printer helped devise a solution where the label could be diecut out and then the resulting puzzle piece could be vacuumed away.

FIRM
Sonsoles

PROJECT
Portfolio

ART DIRECTOR
Sonsoles Llorens

DESIGNER
Sonsoles Llorens

STAND APART

AVOID EXCESS

YOURSELF

FIRM	PROJECT	ART DIRECTOR	DESIGNER
Studiovertex	Self-Promotion Postcard Series	Michael Lindsay	Michael Lindsay

FIRM
Traffic Design
Consultants

PROJECT
Self-Promotion
Portfolio Brochure

ART DIRECTORS
Chris Smith
Scott Witham

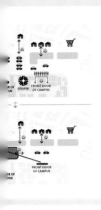

MAKING A
PHYSICAL AND
SYMBOLIC
CONNECTION

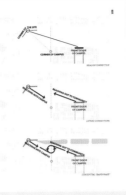

FIRM
Gensler
Los Angeles

PROJECT
ideas_4

ART DIRECTORS
Ben Anderson
Shawn Gehle
Philippe Pare
Li Wen

DESIGNER
Dominick Ricci

SARA SAEDI

sarasaedi.com | saedisara@gmail.com | 310 499 8688

FIRM
Sara Saedi

PROJECT
Handmade
Letterpress Cards

ART DIRECTOR
Sara Saedi

DESIGNER
Sara Saedi

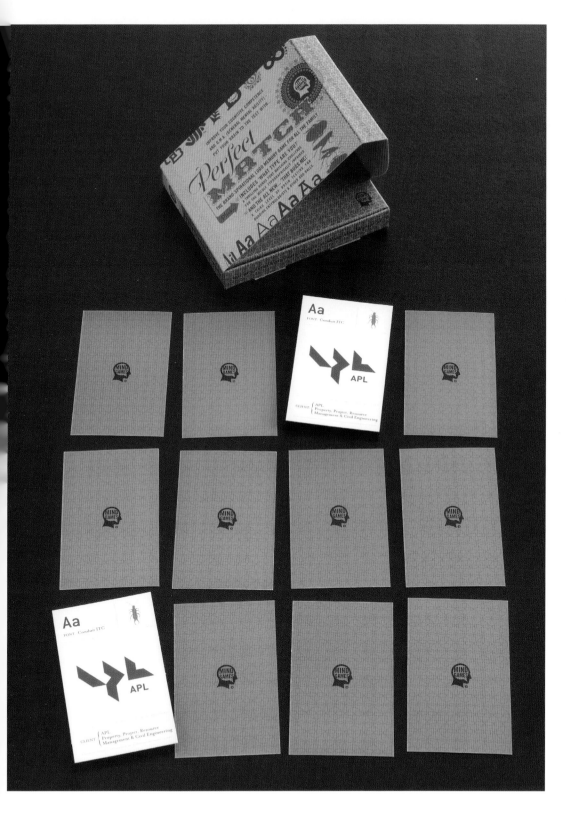

FIRM
Lloyds Graphic
Design Ltd.

PROJECT
Perfect Match
Card Game

ART DIRECTOR
Alexander Lloyd

DESIGNER
Alexander Lloyd

073

Bookmark Me

Thanks for stopping by
today. Please stay in touch
and visit maryquick.com
to stay abreast of my latest
surface design collections.

My collections offer fresh
designs with a wide range of
products and applications
in mind. You'll find natural,
geometric and novelty motifs
that span the seasons and are
always trend-appropriate.

I am always looking for new
opportunities and love
collaborating to bring more
lovely things to life.

Mary Quick
DESIGNS

maryquick.com

Mary Quick
DESIGNS

1015 Overbrook Rd
Baltimore MD 21239
443 522 0853
maryquick.com

FIRM	PROJECT	ART DIRECTOR	DESIGNER
Mary Quick Designs	Pattern Design Trade Show Self-Promotion Kit	Mary Quick	Mary Quick

FIRM
Gilah Press
& Design

PROJECT
Hello Postcards

ART DIRECTOR
Kat Feuerstein

DESIGNER
Nathalie Wilson

FIRM	PROJECT	ART DIRECTOR	DESIGNER
Curious	Curious Work Mailer	Curious	Curious

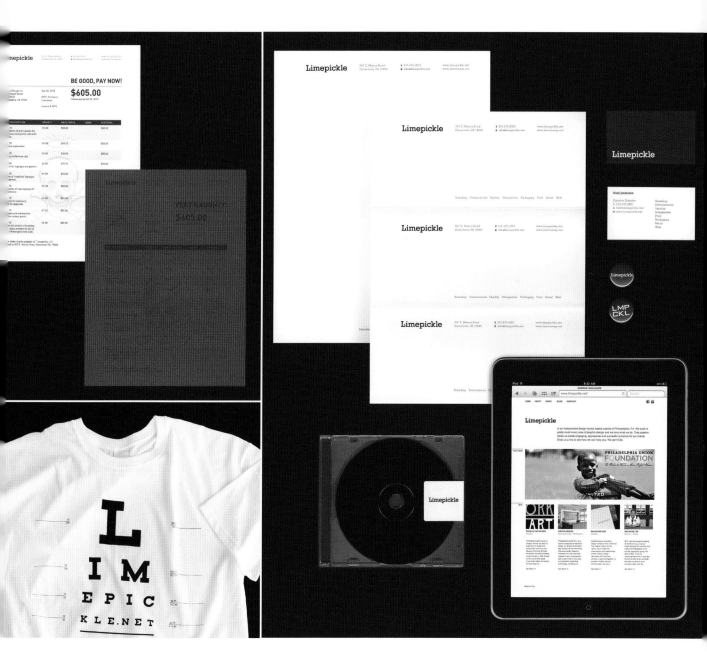

FIRM
LimePickle LLC

PROJECT
Identity &
Stationery Suite

ART DIRECTOR
Mark Jenkinson

DESIGNER
Mark Jenkinson

FIRM
Bruce Mau Design

PROJECT
BMD Studio Book

ART DIRECTOR
Paddy Harrington

DESIGNER
Kar Yan Cheung

Elfen 10

Reversed type
on cover appears
incorrect but leads
to reveal within.

love

Embossed type on the
cover creates a subtle,
textured surface.

Interior printing of
"ve" combined with
the now-debossed
view of "evol" from the
front cover adds a layer
of surprise for those
readers who notice the
word "evolve."

FIRM
Elfen 10

PROJECT
Self-Promotion
Love

volve

ELFEN

For more in
to your busi
then post it b

Name.........

Company........

Address.......

Telephone.......

Email........

Please tick areas of inte
☐   Branding
☐   Graphic Design

Alternatively, you can ca
post@elfen.co.uk or vis

to your

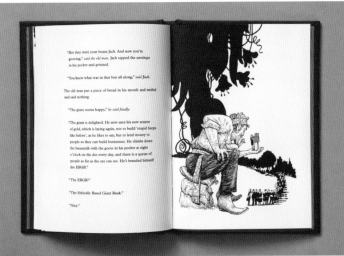

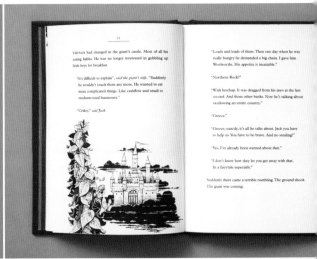

FIRM
The Allotment

PROJECT
Jack and the Giant
Recession

ART DIRECTORS
James Backhurst
Michael Smith

DESIGNER
Michael Smith

"If I'd read this story at the time, I'd have taken the trouble to understand Little Red Riding Hood's needs better, and we could have really got something special going together I think. Instead I ate her. Bad move."

The Wolf

"How frustrating – instead of scoffing that gingerbread house we could have had a successful global food empire! We just didn't realise the potential of our own story."

Hansel

"My story was my strongest asset. If I'd used it wisely I'd never have got in such a rage, never driven my right foot so far into the ground, nor seized my left foot with both hands and torn myself in two. And trust me, tearing yourself in two is not good for growth."

Rumpilstilskin

FIRM
Knock Knock

PROJECT
Clump-o-Lump
Promotion
Mix & Match Book

ART DIRECTOR
Jen Bilik

DESIGNER
Brad Serum

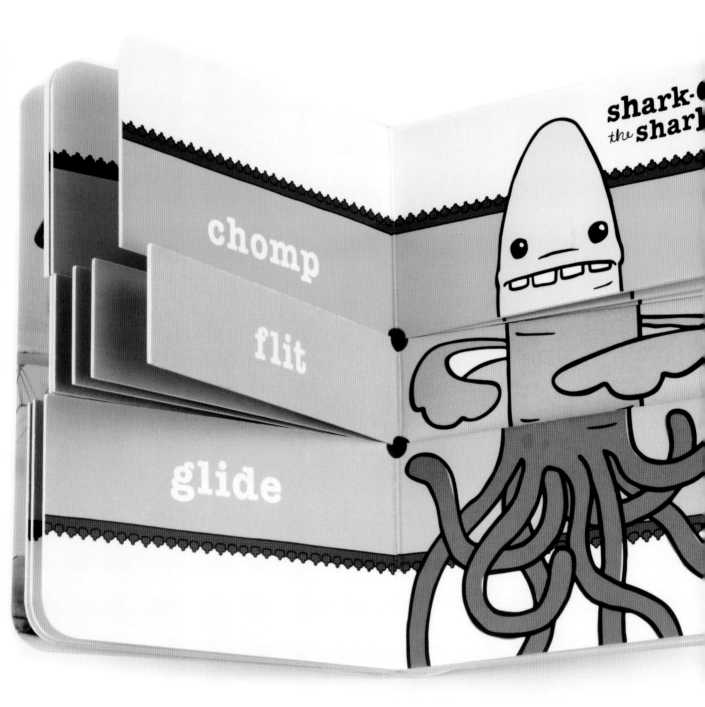

chomp

flit

glide

shark-
the shark

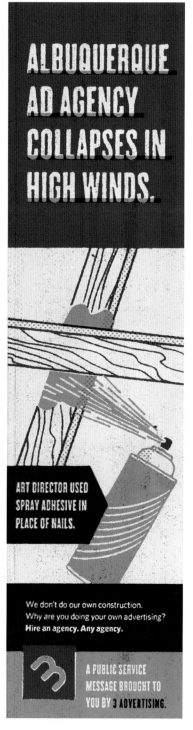

FIRM
3 Advertising

PROJECT
Self-Promotion

ART DIRECTOR
Jesse Arneson

FIRM	**PROJECT**	**ART DIRECTOR**	**DESIGNER**
Fuse Design	Fuse Design Portfolio	Adam Head	Adam Head

DOUG BARTOW
id29, Troy, New York

Get noticed.

One of the biggest shortcomings I see in designers' promotions that make their way to my desk or inbox is the piece simply trying too hard. Visually engaging your target audience is a must, but gratuitously going over the top with production value or plurality of messaging can be detrimental to your strategic objective. All self-promotional projects should begin with you asking yourself: whom do I want to communicate with, and what action do I wish them to take as a result of my efforts. Identifying the types of businesses or organizations of your target audience is critical when you begin organizing your self-promotional effort. Make sure you have proper names and street or email addresses for your recipients, as simply sending the project to "human resources" or "to whom it may concern" is equivalent to throwing your time and money away.

Once you've devised a plan, execute it to the best of your abilities and keep your eye on every detail of the project. If you're producing for print, specify the typefaces, colors, papers, packaging materials and postage stamps used—every detail should be considered to make the project as appealing as possible. Getting your target to actually open the box or envelope is sometimes half the battle in self-promotion. Treating the envelope or outer packaging as just a throw-away piece that doesn't necessarily need to be an integrated part of the project is a good way to get your package filed in the recycling bin before it's ever opened.

The final and most critical step to insuring return on investment for your self-promotional campaign is following up. The target of your efforts may not be actively seeking design help at the exact time they receive your piece. The gestational period for getting noticed and acquiring top-of-mind awareness for your services can be months, and sometimes even years. To keep your awesome-looking design from moving to the bottom of the stack or inbox, follow up with the recipient two weeks after they've received the piece. This can be done via email or phone, or with another clever piece in the same campaign. This will help you filter and revise your mailing list for your next outreach as well. Giddy-up!

Bergman Associates + Mpakt

Thoughtful structure
to the layout is guided
by an underlying
grid to which
the composition
considerations report.

Change of
medium and/
format result
in change of
composition
of content
elements.

FIRM
Bergman
Associates
+ Mpakt

PROJECT
Bergman
Associates Promo
& Billboard

ART DIRECTOR
Robert Bergman

DESIGNER
Alison Munn

Design promotion
in the form of
out-of-home
advertising.

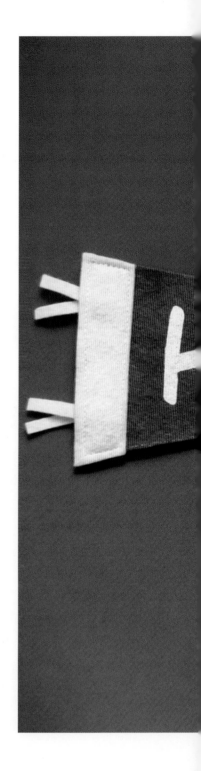

FIRM	PROJECT	ART DIRECTOR	DESIGNER
Christine Blystone	Self-Promotion	Christine Blystone	Christine Blystone

096   Design: Portfolio

FIRM
Marius Fahrner
Design

PROJECT
Stationery

ART DIRECTOR
Marius Fahrner

DESIGNER
Marius Fahrner

„Es ist immer ein großer Moment,
bevor man zu einem völlig neuen
Auftrag geht. Man lüftet Geheim-
nisse und läßt sie Form werden."

MARIUS FAHRNER DESIGN

HAMBURG

„To create, one must first question everything."
EILEEN GREY

MARIUS FAHRNER DESIGN
HAMBURG

www.mariusfahrner.com

FIRM
Marius Fahrner
Design

PROJECT
Portfolio Boxes

ART DIRECTOR
Marius Fahrner

DESIGNER
Marius Fahrner

FIRM
Owen Jones
& Partners

PROJECT
Owen Jones
Paper Suite

ART DIRECTOR
Rusty Grim

DESIGNERS
Dan Christofferson
Mike Henderson
Mark Rawlins
Brandy Shearer

FIRM
Mikey Burton

PROJECT
Inspector Stamp

ART DIRECTOR
Keith Berger

DESIGNER
Mikey Burton

FIRM	**PROJECT**	**ART DIRECTORS**	**DESIGNER**
Better Than One	Oversized Business Cards	Paul Huber John Parsons	Paul Huber

FIRM
Alexander Camlin

PROJECT
Calling Card

DESIGNER
Alexander Camlin

103

FIRM
TOMJ Design

PROJECT
TOMJ Stationery

ART DIRECTOR
Tom Jaeger

DESIGNER
Tom Jaeger

FIRM
The Studio of
Aggie Toppins

PROJECT
"All We Need Is
a Template"

DESIGNER
Aggie Toppins

FIND HAPPINESS IN YOUR WORK.

TAKE NOTE
LEST YOU FORGET

No. 002

FIRM
Wier/Stewart

PROJECT
Wier/Stewart
Stationery Suite

ART DIRECTOR
Daniel Stewart

DESIGNERS
Hannah Elliott
Alex Wier

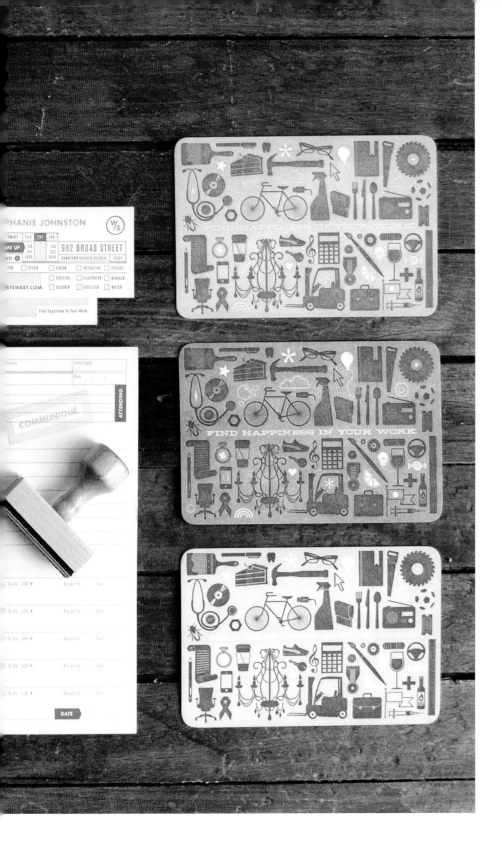

CLOSER LOOK

Ologie

Colorful and
energetic
throughout

A range of objects
that embrace whimsy
and productivity.

FIRM
Ologie

PROJECT
Ologie Campaign—
AMA Higher
Education
Symposium

ART DIRECTORS
Bev Bethge
Andy Hayes
Kelly Ruoff

DESIGNERS
Paul Davis
Kyle Kastranec

Jars, boxes, racks, shelves—variation in displaying pieces

Wide variety of textures, colors, sizes, and shapes helps to keep viewer's interest.

FIRM
Martie Flores

PROJECT
Self-Promotion

DESIGNER
Martie Flores

112   Design: Portfolio

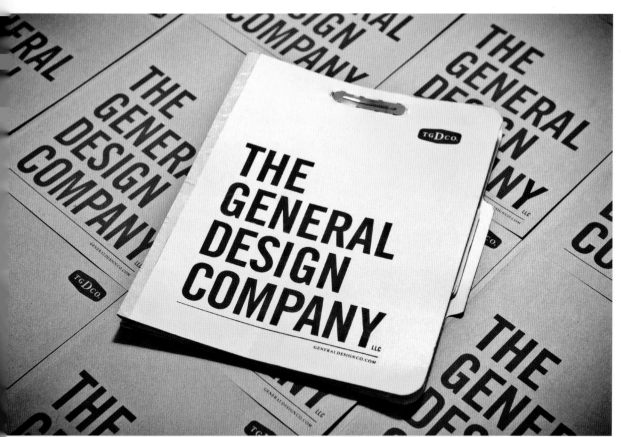

FIRM
The General
Design Company

PROJECT
Brand Collateral

ART DIRECTORS
Scott Livingston
Soung Wiser

DESIGNERS
Scott Livingston
Kaleena Porter
Soung Wiser

CLOSER LOOK

Matter
Strategic
Design

An experiential piece
that creates interest in
and participation from
the recipient.

Subtle in its visual presence but powerful nonetheless.

FIRM
Matter
Strategic Design

PROJECT
Matter 2012
New Year Package

ART DIRECTOR
Mike Kasperski

DESIGNER
Mike Kasperski

Highly focused, two-color treatment creates brand consistency.

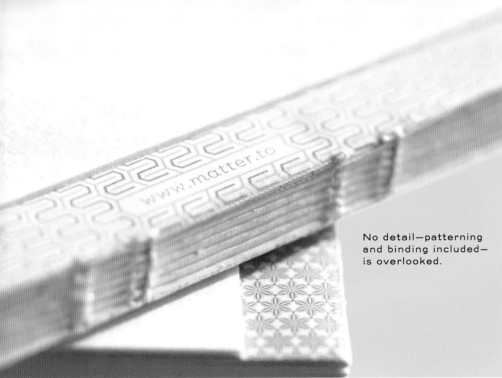

No detail—patterning and binding included— is overlooked.

FIRM	**PROJECT**	**ART DIRECTOR**	**DESIGNERS**
Modern Dog	Westwood	Robynne Ray	Shogo Ota
Design Co.	College Poster		Robynne Raye

FIRM
EME—
Design Studio

PROJECT
Self-Promotional
Posters

ART DIRECTORS
Joel Martinez
Iris Morales

DESIGNER
Iris Morales

A PIECE OF OUR MIND
POSTERS BY JOE SCORSONE & ALICE DRUEDING

FIRM	**PROJECT**	**ART DIRECTORS**	**DESIGNERS**
Scorsone/Drueding	Exhibition Announcement	Joe Scorsone Alice Drueding	Joe Scorsone Alice Drueding

FIRM
Art Chantry

PROJECT
Art Chantry at
Damaged Goods

ART DIRECTOR
Art Chantry

DESIGNER
Art Chantry

121

FIRM
Art Chantry

PROJECT
Rearney NBA 2012

ART DIRECTOR
Art Chantry

DESIGNER
Art Chantry

FIRM
Spunk Design
Machine

PROJECTS
Big Thanks—NYC
Big Thanks—MLPS

ART DIRECTOR
Jeff Johnson

DESIGNERS
Justin Martinez
Lucas Richards

hat-trick

Copy is printed (silkscreened) on both sides of the sheet and registered to align perfectly.

A CARDBOARD PIG,
A SMALL RED BIRD,
ORANGUTANS,
ISAAC NEWTON,
CHEEKY MONKEYS,
DISAFFECTED YOUTH,
PHILATELISTS,
BANANA SKINS,
A GIANT SNAIL,
OLD FARTS,
A HEAD IN A BAG,
SPIDERS,
THE NUMBER THREE,
A FUNNY THING,
HELICOPTERS,
MARINE IGUANAS,
ENORMOUS BRAINS,
TWO JOKERS,
TINY SKETCHBOOKS,
LAVA,
SKYSCRAPERS,
ISAMBARD KINGDOM BRUNEL,
WIND,
RELIGIOUS FANATICS,
THE QUEEN OF SPADES,
POPPIES,
YODA,
A SMALL CREATURE,
LIGHTNING,
DINOSAURS,

two sides of
hat-trick

A talk by
Gareth Howat &
Jim Sutherland

28/01/10
7.00pm

The Typographic Circle
www.typocircle.co.uk

JWT
1 Knightsbridge Green
London SW1X 7NW

Writing plays a
valuable role in
effective design
projects.

125

Translucent stock captures attention even before the piece is unrolled.

typ

two sides of
hat-trick

A talk by
Gareth Howat &
Jim Sutherland

28/01/10
7.00pm

The Typographic Circle
www.typocircle.co.uk

JWT
1 Knightsbridge Green

BOARD PIG,
'ISA 'SMALL
ONKEYS,
DISAFFE
BEE'

FIRM
hat-trick

PROJECT
Typographic
Circle Poster

ART DIRECTORS
Gareth Howat
Jim Sutherland

DESIGNERS
Gareth Howat
Jim Sutherland

hat-trick

Flipped type in the studio's logo has informed the decision to have the poster type running two directions.

FIRM
Bad People
Good Things

PROJECT
Poster for Lecture
at Art Directors
Club of Tulsa

DESIGNER
John Foster

Design Evening
w/ karlssonwilker

Onsdag 13 maj, 20:00
dørene åbner 19:00
entre: 65 dkr, forsalg i
LYNfabrikkens cafe

LYNfabrikken

Vestergade 49B
8000 Aarhus C
www.lynfabrikken.dk

Design Evenings are sponsored by:

FIRM
karlssonwilker

PROJECT
Lecture Posters

ART DIRECTORS
Hjalti Karlsson
Jan Wilker

FIRM
karlssonwilker

PROJECT
Mailer

ART DIRECTORS
Hjalti Karlsson
Jan Wilker

FIRM
Spunk Design
Machine

PROJECT
Sweet 16
Party Poster

ART DIRECTOR
Jeff Johnson

DESIGNER
Lucas Richards

THERE'S NO SCHOOL LIKE THE OLD SCHOOL

THURSDAY APRIL 30TH
6:30 PM - 9:30 PM

SEND AN RSVP EMAIL TO
INFO@GILAHPRESS.COM
BY APRIL 24TH

3506 ASH STREET | BALTIMORE, MARYLAND 21211
INFO@GILAHPRESS.COM | WWW.GILAHPRESS.COM

OPEN HOUSE
GET SCHOOLED.

FIRM
Gilah Press
& Design

PROJECT
Open House
Invitation Poster

ART DIRECTOR
Kat Feuerstein

DESIGNER
Nathalie Wilson

FIRM
Spur Design

PROJECT
Block Style
Poster Mailer

ART DIRECTOR
David Plunkert

DESIGNER
David Plunkert

FIRM	PROJECT	ART DIRECTOR	DESIGNER
Spur Design	Collage Style Poster Mailer	David Plunkert	David Plunkert

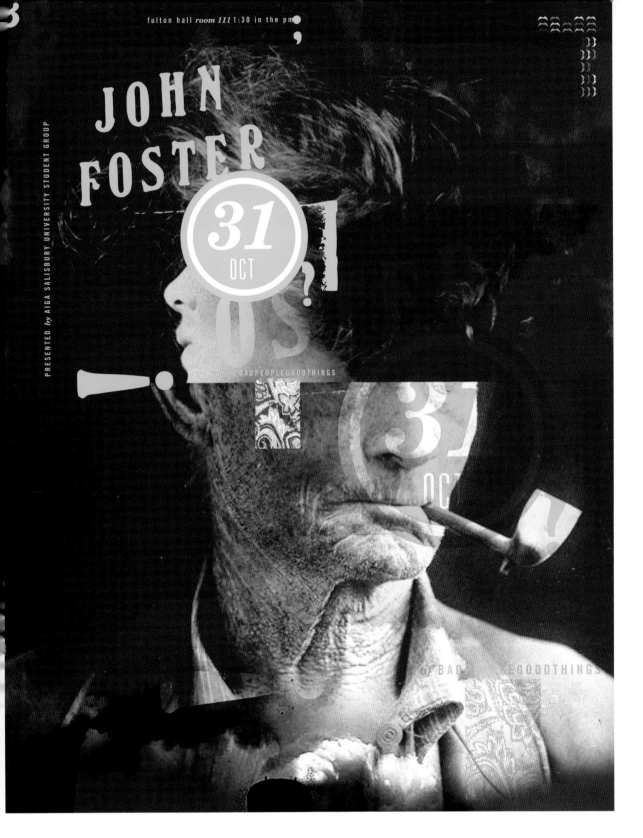

FIRM
Bad People
Good Things

PROJECT
Poster for Lecture
at Salisbury
University

DESIGNER
John Foster

...MATTEO•BOLOGNA

...MUCCA•DESIGN...

28 OCTOBER 2011...

...BOO4•1:00pm...

MATTEO BOLOGNA · MUCCA DESIGN presented by GRAPHIC AND INTERACTIVE DESIGN

TYLER SCHOOL OF ART · TEMPLE UNIVERSITY · 28 OCTOBER 2011 · ALL ARE WELCOME

THIS PROGRAM IS MADE POSSIBLE THROUGH THE USE OF GENERAL ACTIVITIES FEES.

FIRM
Tyler School
of Art

PROJECT
Mucca Design
Lecture
Promotion

DESIGNER
Kelly Holohan

FIRM
Tyler School
of Art

PROJECT
Paula Scher
Lecture
Promotion

DESIGNER
Kelly Holohan

SO MANY BOOKS, SO LITTLE TIME

Roberto de Vicq de Cumptich

{prolific designer *of* books & more}

Friday · March 19 · 2010
Tyler School of Art · Temple University
2:00 pm · Room 240B

sponsored by the Graphic & Interactive Design (GAID) Department

TYLER SCHOOL OF ART *of* TEMPLE UNIVERSITY · 2001 NORTH 13TH STREET · PHILADELPHIA · PENNSYLVANIA 19122

FIRM
Tyler School
of Art

PROJECT
Roberto de Vicq
Lecture
Promotion

DESIGNER
Kelly Holohan

FIRM
hat-trick

PROJECT
Lecture Posters

ART DIRECTORS
Gareth Howat
Jim Sutherland

DESIGNER
Jim Sutherland

FIRM	**PROJECT**	**ART DIRECTOR**	**DESIGNER**
CF Napa	99 Bottles of Wine Poster	David Schuemann	Dana Deininger

FIRM
J Fletcher Design

PROJECT
Icons Promo Print

DESIGNER
Jay Fletcher

FIRM
Alex Robbins
Studio

PROJECT
Keep Me Busy
Postcard

ART DIRECTOR
Alex Robbins

DESIGNER
Alex Robbins

KNOCK KNOCK'S TRADESHOW

ALL OUT OF

☐ MOJO ☐ ASPIRIN ☐ WITTY RETORT
☐ SMILES ☐ BREATH MINTS ☐ MONEY
☐ CAFFEINE ☐ COURTESY ☐ COOL WARES

NOTES:

VISIT KNOCK KNOCK—STOCK UP AND FEEL BETTER!

FIRM	PROJECT	ART DIRECTOR	DESIGNER
Knock Knock	Tradeshow Promo— Sticky Note	Trish Abbot	Brad Serum

CLOSER LOOK

Lorenzo Petrantoni

Typography via
assemblage

Shadowing across the surface from the individual elements adds dimension to an otherwise flat set of content.

Scale of the commitment required speaks to the value of the design.

FIRM
Lorenzo Petrantoni

PROJECT
Exposition

ART DIRECTOR
Lorenzo Petrantoni

DESIGNER
Lorenzo Petrantoni

Compositional masterpiece with a consistent density of black and white provides a sense of balance.

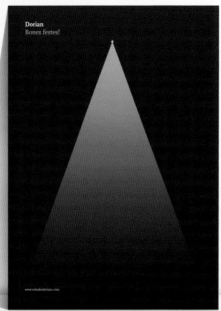

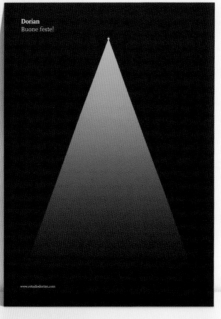

FIRM
Dorian

PROJECT
The Studio's
Greetings
for 2012

Dorian
Joyeuses fêtes!

www.estudiodorian.com

FIRM
Orange Element

PROJECT
Work Smarter
Posters

ART DIRECTOR
Andrea Campbell

DESIGNERS
Andy Bonner
Dave Colson
Nicolette Cornelius
Kuoting Lian

FIRM
Creature

PROJECT
Year of the Rabbit
Poster

ART DIRECTOR
Steve Cullen

DESIGNER
Shawn Diaz

FIRM	**PROJECT**	**ART DIRECTOR**	**DESIGNERS**
Airtype Studio	Letterpress	Bryan Ledbetter	Adam Dixon
	Coasters		Bryan Ledbetter

FIRM	PROJECT	ART DIRECTOR	DESIGNERS
Nemo Design	Holiday Insurgency Kit	Jeff Bartel	Thomas Bradley
			Ryan Davis
			Mike Schwoebel
			Kris Seymour

FALLING LEAVES

FIRM
Wallace
Church, Inc.

PROJECT
Thanksgiving Wine
Falling Leaves

ART DIRECTOR
Stan Church

DESIGNER
Akira Yasuda

Anthropologie

Fabric and thread
add texture while the
closure adds a touch
of expectation.

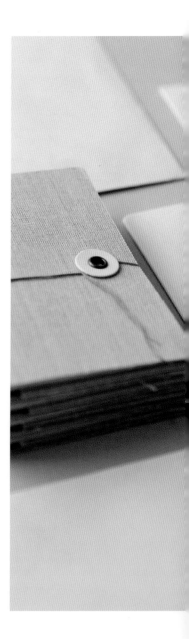

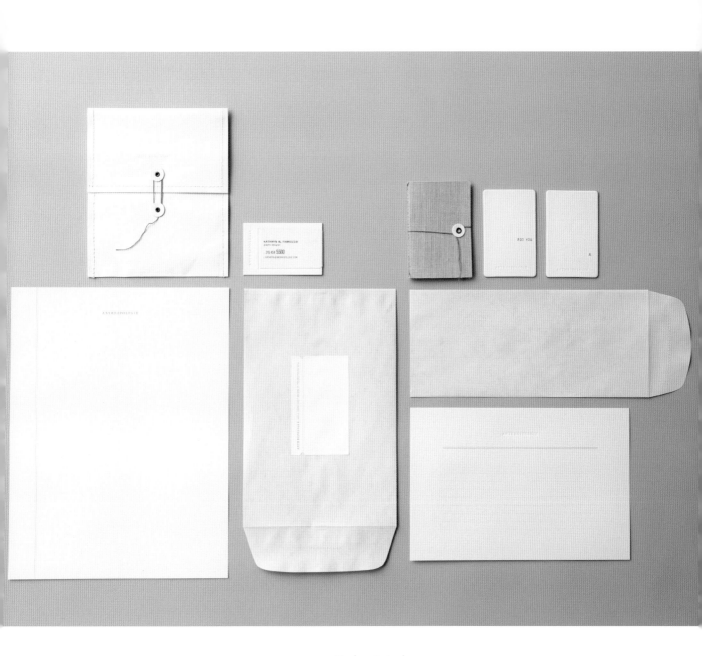

Understated
color palette adds
sophistication and
assuredness.

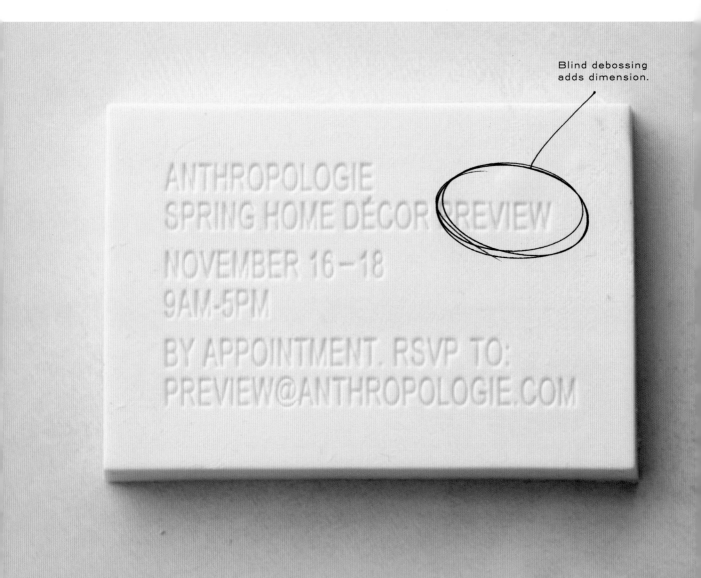

Blind debossing adds dimension.

ANTHROPOLOGIE
SPRING HOME DÉCOR PREVIEW
NOVEMBER 16–18
9AM-5PM

BY APPOINTMENT. RSVP TO:
PREVIEW@ANTHROPOLOGIE.COM

FIRM
Anthropologie

PROJECTS
Identity System
& Press Event
Promotions

ART DIRECTOR
Carolyn Keer

DESIGNERS
Kathryn Fabrizio
Alana McCann

ANTHROPOLOGIE
FALL 2010 HOME DÉCOR PREVIEW

MAY 11 TO 13

9 TO 5 PM

FOR APPOINTMENTS, CONTACT:
PREVIEW@ANTHROPOLOGIE.COM
OR CALL 646.728.2155

Colored felt filler
adds playfulness.

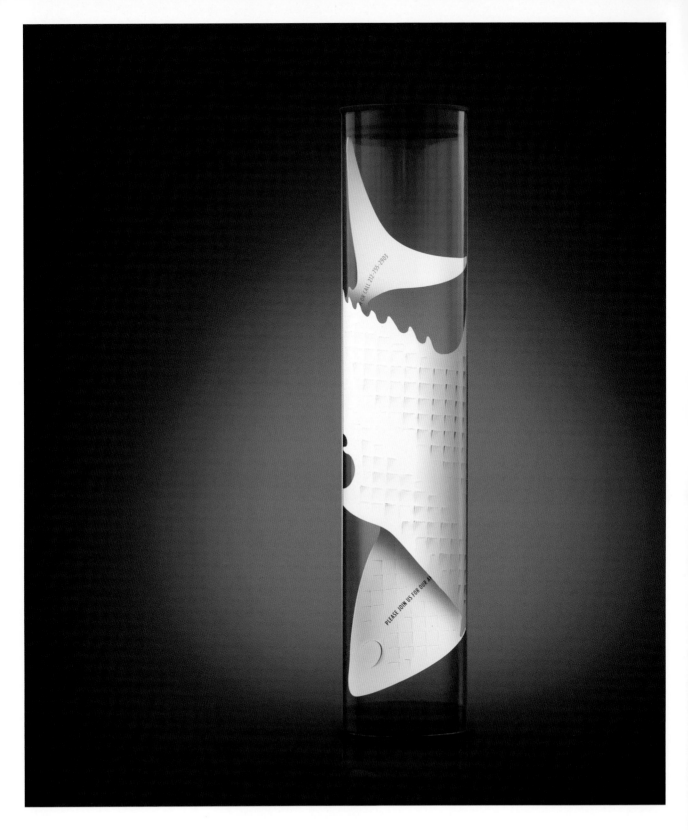

FIRM
Wallace
Church, Inc.

PROJECT
Tuna Invite 2010

ART DIRECTOR
Stan Church

DESIGNER
Becca Reiter

Face.
Secret—
Ideas.

Face.
Recycled-
Dossier.

Face.
Simple—
Bag.

DesignByFace.Com

FIRM	PROJECT	ART DIRECTOR	DESIGNER
Face.	Branding and Stationery Material	Face.	Face.

FIRM
End of Work

PROJECT
Wine Packaging

ART DIRECTOR
Justin Smith

DESIGNER
Justin Smith

FIRM	PROJECT	ART DIRECTORS	DESIGNERS
Spur Design	Illustration	Joyce Hesselberth	Joyce Hesselberth
	Portfolio Promos	David Plunkert	David Plunkert

FIRM
Knock Knock

PROJECT
Trade Show
Promo Pen

ART DIRECTOR
Trish Abbot

DESIGNER
Brad Serum

FIRM
3 Advertising

PROJECT
3 Advertising
Holiday Survival Kit

ART DIRECTOR
Jesse Arneson

165

FIRM
Gilah Press
& Design

PROJECT
Trade Show
Giveaway—
Cootie Catcher

ART DIRECTOR
Kat Feuerstein

DESIGNER
Nathalie Wilson

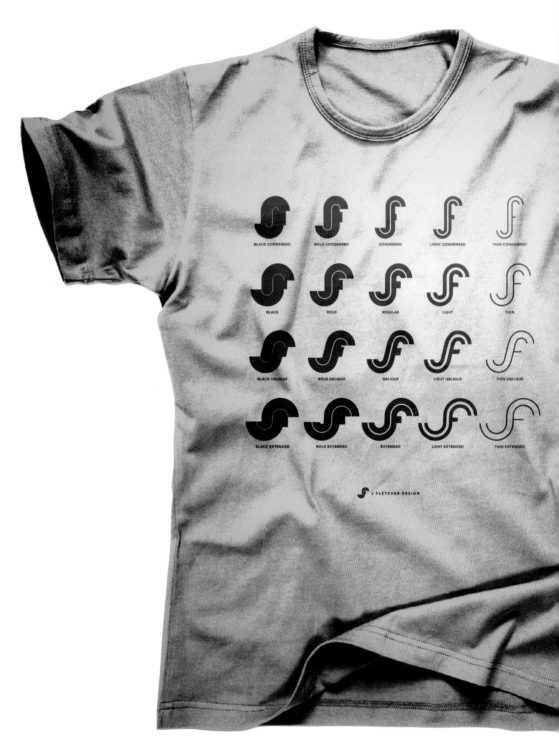

BLACK CONDENSED   BOLD CONDENSED   CONDENSED   LIGHT CONDENSED   THIN CONDENSED

BLACK   BOLD   REGULAR   LIGHT   THIN

BLACK OBLIQUE   BOLD OBLIQUE   OBLIQUE   LIGHT OBLIQUE   THIN OBLIQUE

BLACK EXTENDED   BOLD EXTENDED   EXTENDED   LIGHT EXTENDED   THIN EXTENDED

J FLETCHER DESIGN

FIRM
J Fletcher Design

PROJECT
What's Your Type?

DESIGNER
Jay Fletcher

RoAndCo Studio

Consistency from packaging to print

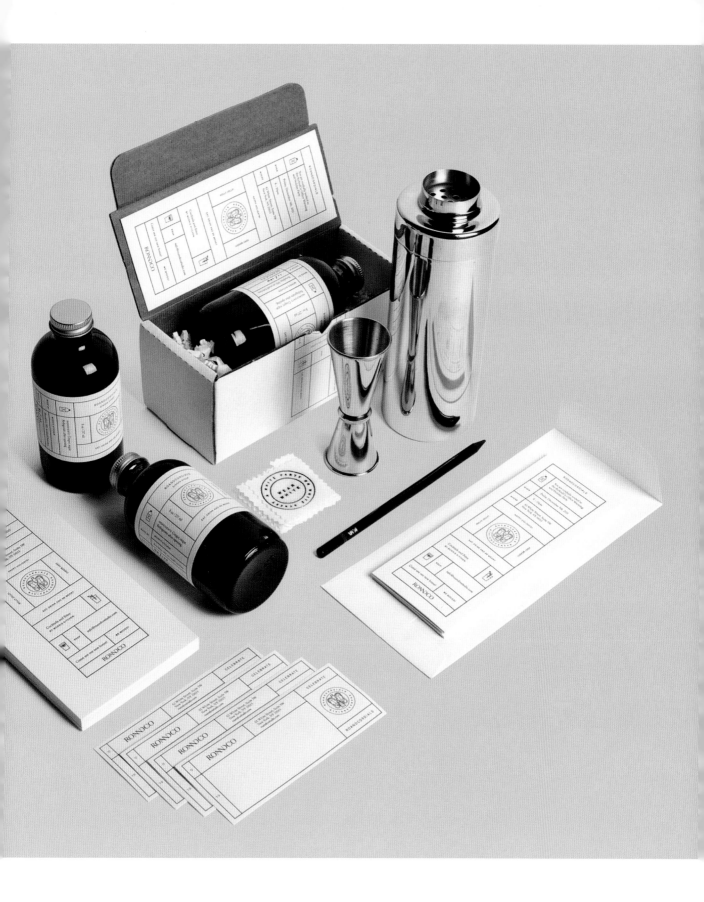

White as the core color ties
in nicely with the event theme,
"A White Party on White Street."

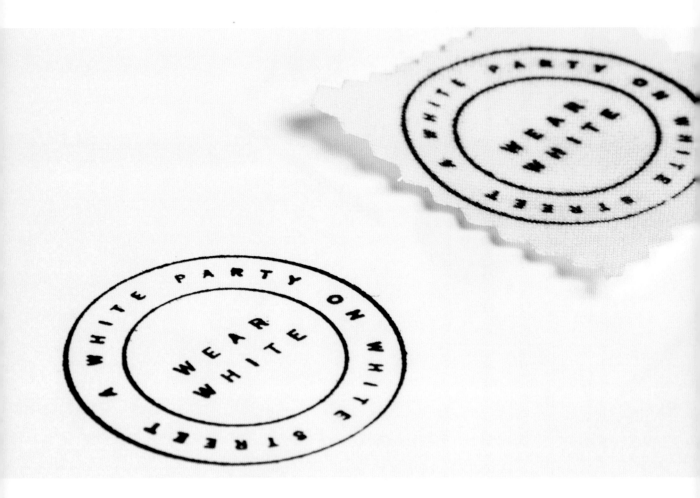

FIRM
RoAndCo Studio

PROJECT
Party

ART DIRECTOR
Roanne Adams

DESIGNER
Lotta Neiminen

Gridded content areas provide structure and formality.

ROANDCORDIALS

You are cordially invited to the RoAndCo Office Warming and Holiday Party

Friday, December 9th, 2011

8 – 10pm

WHEN

62 White Street, Suite 3W
New York, NY 10013

WHERE

HAPPY HOLIDAYS!

VERY

ROANDCORDIALS
GINGER SYRUP

8 oz / 237 ml

INGREDIENTS Ginger, sugar

EAT, DRINK, AND BE MERRY

ROANDCORDIALS
GINGER SYRUP

8 oz / 237 ml

EAT, DRINK AND BE MERRY

INGREDIENTS Ginger, sugar.
Refrigerate after opening.

MADE BY   MORRIS KITCHEN

Brooklyn, NY, in small batches

BATCH N°   52 / 100

RO

FIRM
Red Antler

PROJECT
Client Holiday Gift

ART DIRECTOR
Simon Endres

DESIGNERS
Simon Endres
Goodship Totes

FIRM	PROJECT	ART DIRECTOR	DESIGNERS
Alt Group	Alt Xmas 2010	Dean Poole	Clem Devine Dean Poole Tony Proffit

FIRM
Wier/Stewart

PROJECT
Peanuts

ART DIRECTOR
Daniel Stewart

DESIGNER
Alex Wier

FIRM
Wallace
Church, Inc.

PROJECT
Tuna Invite 2012

ART DIRECTOR
Stan Church

DESIGNER
Stan Church

THREE SHEEPS TO THE WIND

FIRM	**PROJECT**	**ART DIRECTOR**	**DESIGNER**
Wallace Church, Inc.	Three Sheeps to the Wind	Stan Church	Stan Church

IRM
End of Work

PROJECT
Death to Average
Gift Sacks

ART DIRECTOR
Justin Smith

DESIGNERS
Bec Macdonald
Goran Momircevski
Justin Smith

FIRM
Gilah Press
& Design

PROJECT
Trade Show
Giveaway—
Gilah Equipment
Coasters

ART DIRECTOR
Kat Feuerstein

DESIGNER
Nathalie Wilson

FIRM
Egg Creatives
PTE Ltd

PROJECT
Christmas 2012
Bottles

ART DIRECTOR
Jason Chen

DESIGNER
Cheryl Chna

FIRM
Knock Knock

PROJECT
Trade Show
Promo Bracelets

ART DIRECTOR
Trish Abbot

DESIGNER
Brad Serum

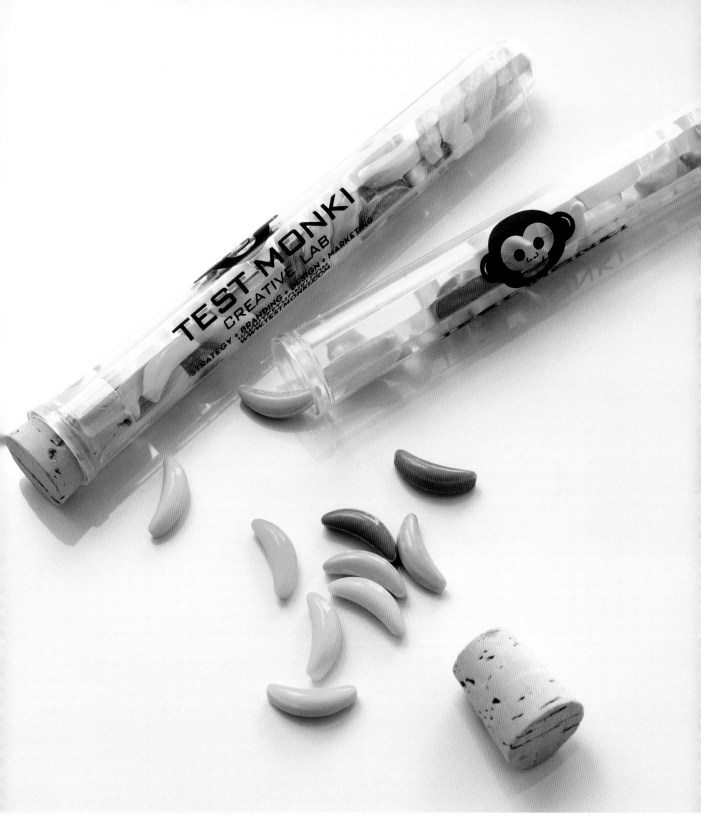

FIRM
Test Monki

PROJECT
Test Tubes

ART DIRECTOR
Suzy Simmons

181

KesselsKramer

Wide range of styles, objects,
printed matter, websites

Underlying sense of
positivity throughout

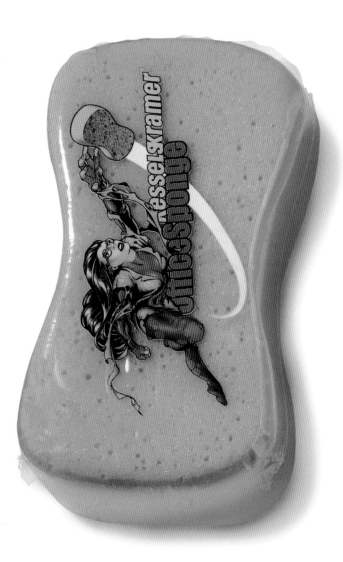

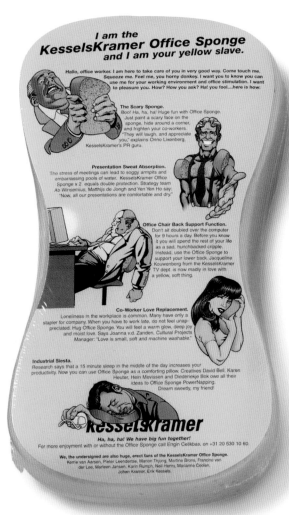

A design voice that is
playful and unexpected

coming soon:
2 kilo
of kesselskramer

just arrived:
2 kilo
of kesselskramer

out now:
2 kilo
of kesselskramer

Variation leads to
a consistent design
approach.

FIRM
Bedow

PROJECT
Mikkeller + Bedow
Packaging

ART DIRECTOR
Perniclas Bedow

DESIGNER
Anders Bollman

FIRM	PROJECT	ART DIRECTORS	DESIGNERS
Good Fucking Design Advice	Erasers	Jason Bacher Brian Buirge	Jason Bacher Brian Buirge

FIRM
MDG

PROJECT
Fresh Air Mailer

ART DIRECTOR
Tim Merry

DESIGNER
Kris Greene

FIRM
Timber Design Co.

PROJECT
Outdoor
Adventure Promo

ART DIRECTOR
Lars Lawson

189

FIRM
Audrie Kapinus

PROJECT
New Year's Theme
Wine Bottle

ART DIRECTOR
Kristin Breslin
Sommese

DESIGNER
Audrie Kapinus

FIRM
Graphic Design
Studio by Yurko
Gutsulyak

PROJECT
Trash Calendar

ART DIRECTOR
Yurko Gutsalyuk

DESIGNER
Yurko Gutsalyuk

Thomas
Printers

Circular format
is engaging in a
rectangular world.

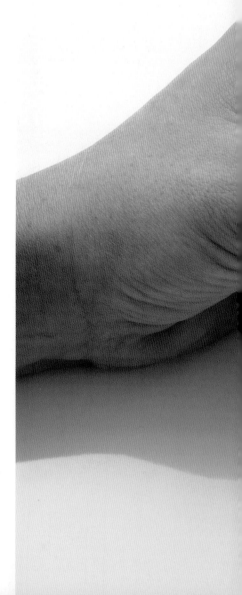

Grommet in center is a
visual accent around which
content is presented.

CRAFTSMANSHIP

MOTTO

CUSTOM

thomas-printers
letterpress printing & design

kseniya@thomas-printers.com
www.thomas-printers.com
www.yonderyes!.com

no two
are alike...

the
LETTERPRESS WHEEL
of
LIBERATING LABORS
and
PRAGMATIC PROCESSES

GREETINGS

EXPERIENCE

METHOD

CRAFTSMANSHIP

CUSTOM

MOTTO

no TWO
are alike...

the SQUEAKY
wheel gets...

GREETINGS

LETTERPRESS

Send a
GOOD word.

Send some love!

INVITATIONS

TRIUMPHANT!

Trust in us!

FAST and good!

EXPERIENCE

METHOD

Key words lead to
expressive statements
and visuals that
summarize the
company's voice.

FIRM
Thomas Printers

PROJECT
Wheel Promotion

ART DIRECTOR
Kseniya Thomas

DESIGNER
Chris Stamas

Dimensional quality
of letterpress further
enhanced by layering
of thick paper stock.

195

FIRM
Lead Graffiti

PROJECT
Tour de Lead
Graffiti 2011
Clamshell Portfolio

ART DIRECTORS
Jill Cypher
Ray Nichols

DESIGNERS
Jill Cypher
Ray Nichols
Tray Nichols

IRM	**PROJECT**	**ART DIRECTORS**	**DESIGNERS**
Lead Graffiti	Postcard	Jill Cypher	Jill Cypher
	Portfolio Projects	Ray Nichols	Ray Nichols
			Tray Nichols

ROBYNNE RAYE
Modern Dog, Seattle, Washington

Boundaries
of Taste

Before the Internet, designers had to rely on physical portfolios to promote themselves. In 1991, my three-person design studio was a struggling five-year-old going through growing pains. We knew we had to figure out some way to increase our income.

Up until that point, we had been mostly working with nonprofits in the arts. We knew we needed to attract clients with bigger budgets in order to keep working for the non-profits, but we weren't sure exactly how to make that transition from charging $250 for a logo to getting paid $15,000 for one. We knew we needed to make some noise.

With our limited resources, we designed and built ten fur box portfolios. Each box, customized to hold our design samples, proved to be a litmus test for potential new clients. We were intentional in the approach, and knew they would either love it or hate it. The box was covered in synthetic dog fur material of varying colors and lengths and wrapped with a studded dog collar sporting a metal bone tag. The tag read:

We then lined the box with a fake newspaper—designed and written by my business partner. It was a mixing of design, dogs and cars-for-sale humor. Each box was custom filled to cater specifically to our target prospects.

And it worked. The ten boxes we sent out yielded several phone calls. One recipient called just to let us know she screamed when she opened it because she thought we had sent her a dead animal. More importantly, it brought us two new clients. Wieden+Kennedy hired us to design ads for Nike Kids, and another got our foot in the door at Warner Bros. Records, where we began designing music industry promotions and CD packaging. That relationship lasted for five-plus years.

The box was held in disdain by some people in the design industry. When we entered it into several design industry competitions, it was singled out by more than one person who asserted that this was not what design was about. And we were okay with that because we were a tiny company of nobodies, and we were singled out and it got people talking about us. We even got requests for more boxes from people who read about us in articles.

Every designer creates their own boundaries. For us, it was important to take risks and be clear about our intent. More than two decades later, as I reflect back, I have to admit that it was much easier for us to take that risk because we had nothing to lose. I also recognize that one furry box single-handedly shaped a key part of our careers and set a rather whimsical precedent for the people who hired us.

FIRM
3 Advertising

PROJECT
Mayan Calendar—
Cats of the
Apocalypse

ART DIRECTOR
Jessa Arneson

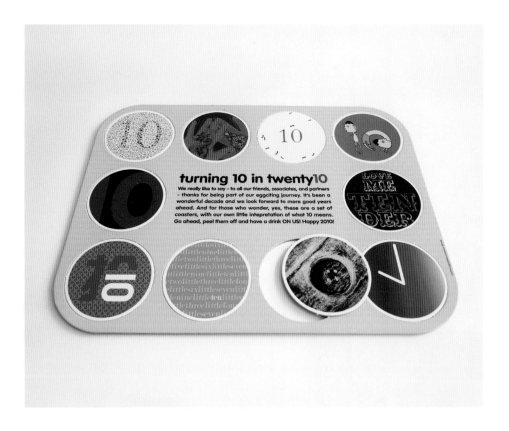

FIRM
Egg Creatives PTE
LTD

PROJECT
10th Anniversary
Coasters

ART DIRECTOR
Jason Chen

DESIGNER
Egg Creative Team

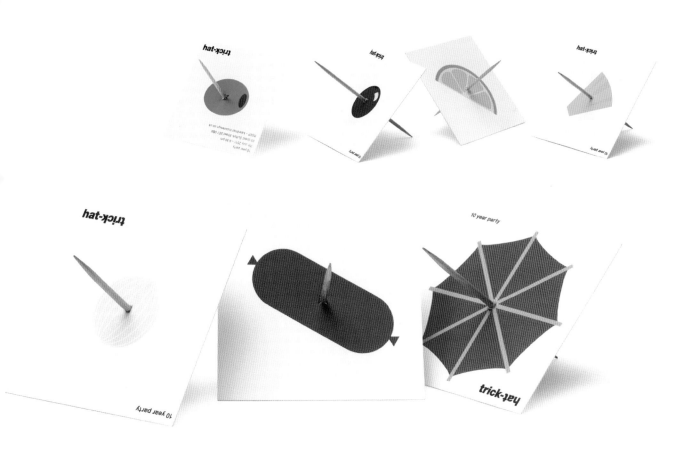

FIRM
hat-trick

PROJECT
Cocktail Party
Invitation

ART DIRECTORS
Gareth Howat
Jim Sutherland

DESIGNER
Laura Bowman

Yellow Octopus PTE Ltd

Calendar days
displayed horizontally.

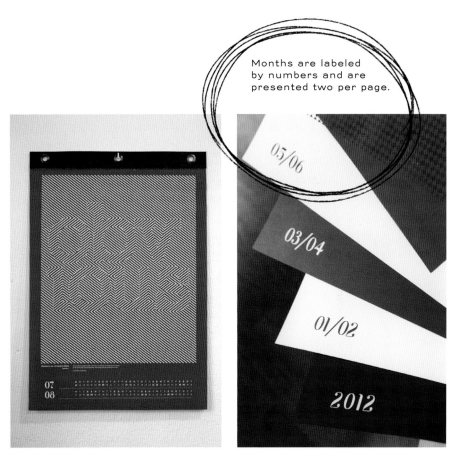

Months are labeled by numbers and are presented two per page.

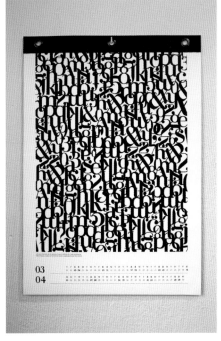

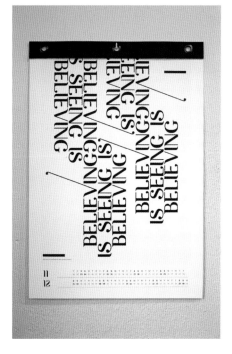

Black, white, and red color palette is as crisp as the graphics.

FIRM
Yellow Octopus
PTE Ltd

PROJECT
Yellow Octopus
Calendar

ART DIRECTORS
Kevin Thio
Jason Chua

DESIGNER
Lau Shu Hui

Grommets add an
industrial sense—
getting things done.

Layering of diecut
typography on printed
typography

FIRM
Wallace
Church, Inc.

PROJECT
US Open Invitation

ART DIRECTOR
Stan Church

DESIGNERS
Stan Church
Chung-Tao Tu

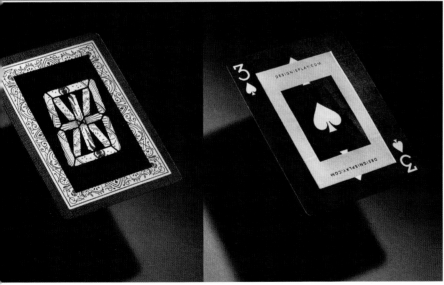

FIRM
Design Is Play

PROJECT
Website
Announcement

DESIGNERS
Mark Fox
Angie Wang

FIRM
Owen Jones
& Partners

PROJECT
Owen Jones
Postcard

ART DIRECTORS
Rusty Grim
Mark Rawlins

DESIGNER
Mark Rawlins

FIRM	PROJECT	ART DIRECTOR	DESIGNERS
Wallace Church, Inc.	35th Anniversary Promo	Stan Church	Wallace Church Design Team

FIRM	PROJECT	ART DIRECTOR	DESIGNER
Studio on Fire	Saw Blades	Studio on Fire	Studio on Fire

FIRM	PROJECT	ART DIRECTOR	DESIGNER
Studio on Fire	Studio on Fire 2012 Letterpress Calendar	Studio on Fire	Studio on Fire

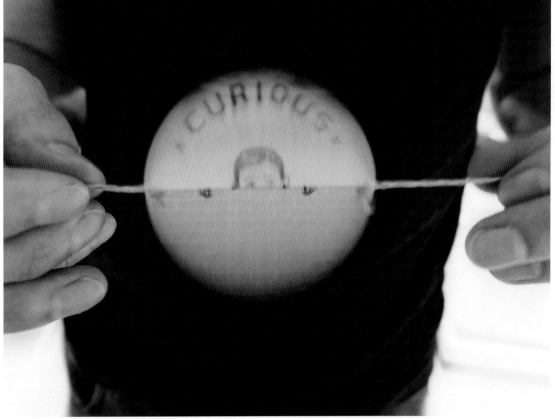

FIRM	PROJECT	ART DIRECTOR	DESIGNER
Curious	Christmas Thaumatropes	Curious	Curious

FIRM
Wallace
Church, Inc.

PROJECT
Tuna Invite 2011

ART DIRECTOR
Stan Church

DESIGNER
Stan Church

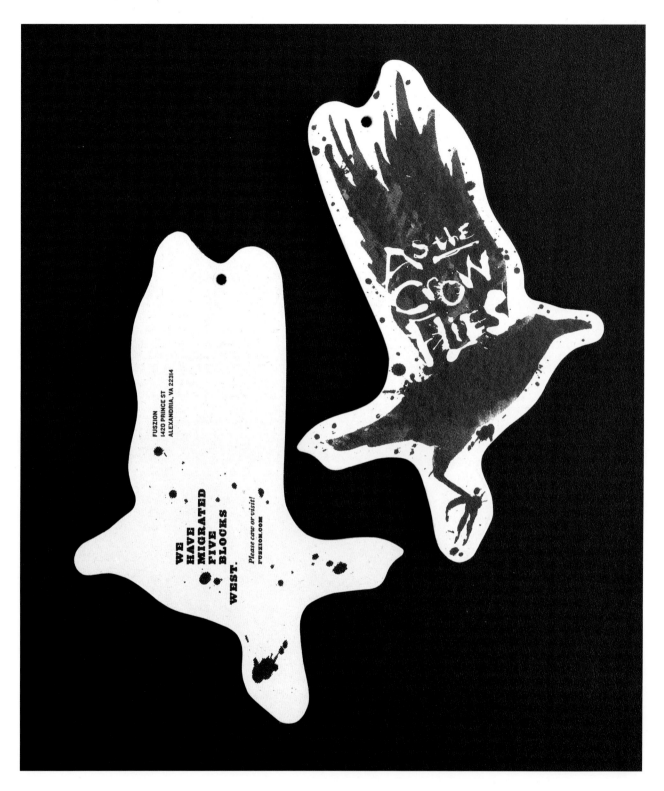

FUSZION
1420 PRINCE ST
ALEXANDRIA, VA 22314

WE HAVE MIGRATED FIVE BLOCKS WEST.

Please caw or visit!
FUSZION.COM

As the Crow Flies

FIRM
Fuszion

PROJECT
"As the Crow Flies"
Moving
Announcement

ART DIRECTOR
Rick Heffner

DESIGNER
Dan Deli-Colli

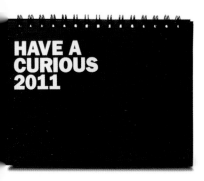

**HAVE A
CURIOUS
2011**

**CURIOUS
FEBRUARY**

M	T	W	T	F	S	S
	01	02	03	04	**05**	**06**
07	08	09	10	11	**12**	**13**
14	15	16	17	18	**19**	**20**
21	22	23	24	25	**26**	**27**
28						

2nd   Ground Hog Day

11th   National Doodle Day

27th   No Brainer Day

www.curiouslondon.com

**CURIOUS
MARCH**

M	T	W	T	F	S	S
	01	02	03	04	**05**	**06**
07	08	09	10	11	**12**	**13**
14	15	16	17	18	**19**	**20**
21	22	23	24	25	**26**	**27**
28	29	30	31			

3rd   If Pets Had Thumbs Day

13th   Ear Muff Day

14th   International Ask A Question Day

www.curiouslondon.com

**CURIOUS
MAY**

M	T	W	T	F	S	S
						01
02	03	04	05	06	**07**	**08**
09	10	11	12	13	**14**	**15**
16	17	18	19	20	**21**	**22**
23	24	25	26	27	**28**	**29**
30	31					

8th   Stay Up All Night Day

16th   National Sea Monkey Day

22nd Buy A Musical Instrument Day

www.curiouslondon.com

**CURIOUS
JUNE**

M	T	W	T	F	S	S
		01	02	03	**04**	**05**
06	07	08	09	10	**11**	**12**
13	14	15	16	17	**18**	**19**
20	21	22	23	24	**25**	**26**
27	28	29	30			

1st   National Barefoot Day

2nd   Leave The Office Early Day

6th   National Yo-yo Day

www.curiouslondon.com

**CURIOUS
OCTOBER**

M	T	W	T	F	S	S
					01	**02**
03	04	05	06	07	**08**	**09**
10	11	12	13	14	**15**	**16**
17	18	19	20	21	**22**	**23**
24	25	26	27	28	**29**	**30**
31						

9th   Curious Events Day

12th   International Moment
        Of Frustration Day

25th   Punk For A Day Day

www.curiouslondon.com

FIRM	PROJECT	ART DIRECTOR	DESIGNER
Curious	Calendar 2011	Curious	Curious

FIRM	PROJECT	ART DIRECTOR	DESIGNER
Sonsoles	New Year Promotion	Sonsoles Llorens	Sonsoles Llorens

FIRM
Flywheel Design

PROJECT
Splash Mob
Public Water Fight
in Downtown
Durham

ART DIRECTOR
Woody Holliman

DESIGNER
Nicole Kraieski

FIRM
Justin Colt

PROJECT
Holiday Mailer

ART DIRECTOR
Justin Colt

DESIGNER
Justin Colt

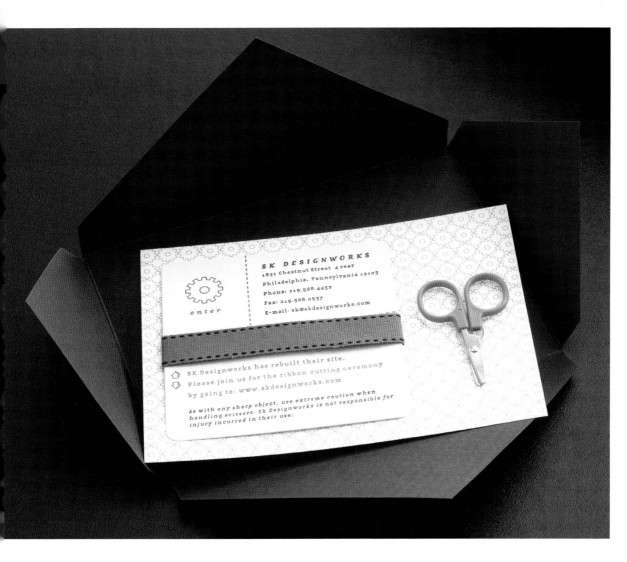

FIRM
SK Designworks

PROJECT
Website Promotion

ART DIRECTOR
Soonduk Krebs

DESIGNER
Vicki Gray

FIRM	PROJECT	ART DIRECTORS	DESIGNER
Hatch Design	5th Annual Egg-Coloring Kit	Katie Jain Joel Templin	Will Ecke

FIRM	**PROJECT**	**ART DIRECTORS**	**DESIGNER**
Hatch Design	4th Annual Egg-Coloring Kit	Katie Jain Joel Templin	Jeffrey Bucholtz

Hatch Design

Form of
dimensional
object mirror
forms and
proportions
of printed
illustrations.

TOGETHER, BEAUTIFUL THINGS ARE POSSIBLE. Hatch 4/5/12

Blind debossing adds subtle shadowing and dimension.

Typography extends
to space within the
vertical stem of the H.

SF
CA

Hatch anniver

Dimensional wood
with laser etching

FIRM
Hatch Design

PROJECT
5th Anniversary
Invitation

ART DIRECTORS
Katie Jain
Joel Templin

DESIGNER
Eszter Clark

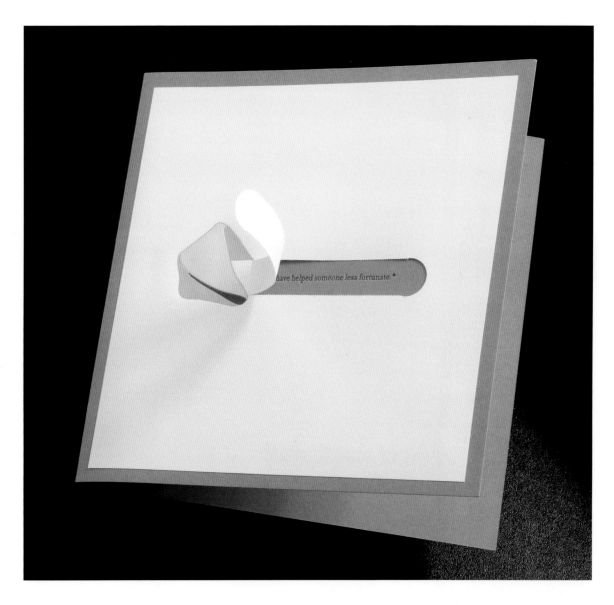

have helped someone less fortunate. *

FIRM
Gilah Press
& Design

PROJECT
Holiday Card

ART DIRECTOR
Kat Feuerstein

DESIGNERS
Kat Feuerstein
Ahn Hee Strain

228   Design: Portfolio

CHEER

GOOD FORTUNE

LOVE PEACE

JOY

LOCAL PROJECTS INVITES YOU TO SPREAD SOME CHEER THIS HOLIDAY SEASON!

FOES OR STRANGERS

GOOD FORTUNE IS LIKE A LETTER:
IT NEEDS TO BE SENT BEFORE IT IS RECEIVED.

THE GIFT THAT KEEPS ON GIVING

TO: _____
FROM: _____

_____
_____
_____
_____

FIRM	PROJECT	ART DIRECTOR	DESIGNER
Local Projects	2010 Holiday Card	Katie Lee	Claire Lin

FIRM
Real Fresh
Creative

PROJECT
Hoppy Halidays
Ornament/Coaster

ART DIRECTOR
Kayle Simon

DESIGNER
Kayle SImon

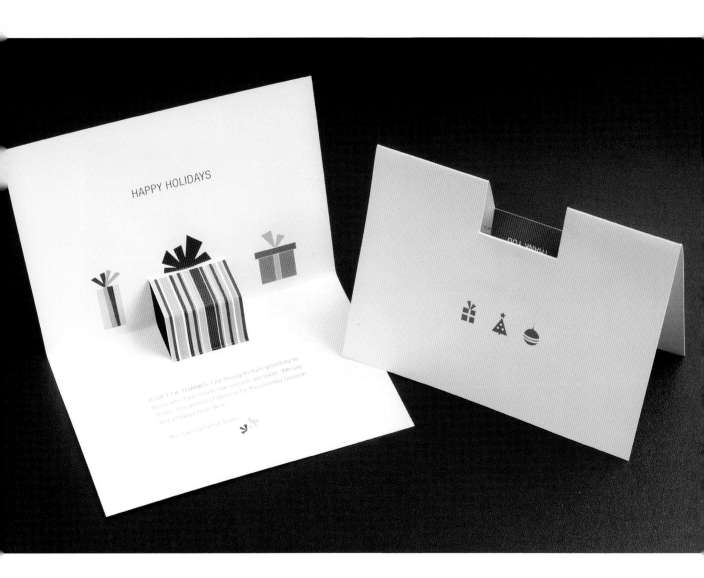

HAPPY HOLIDAYS

A GIFT OF THANKS. Our thoughts turn gratefully to
those who have made our success possible. We say
Thank You and Best Wishes for the Holiday Season
and a Happy New Year.

FIRM
substance151

PROJECT
Holiday Cards

ART DIRECTOR
Ida Cheinman

DESIGNERS
Ida Cheinman
Rick Salzman

FIRM
Willoughby Design

PROJECT
Willo Sweets—
Valentine's Day
Gifts

ART DIRECTORS
Ann Willoughby
Nicole Satterwhite

DESIGNERS
Roberto Camacho
Becky Ediger
Nicole Satterwhite

FIRM
Local Projects

PROJECT
2011 Holiday Card

ART DIRECTORS
Ian Curry
Katie Lee

DESIGNERS
Greg Mihalko
Hannah Schwartz

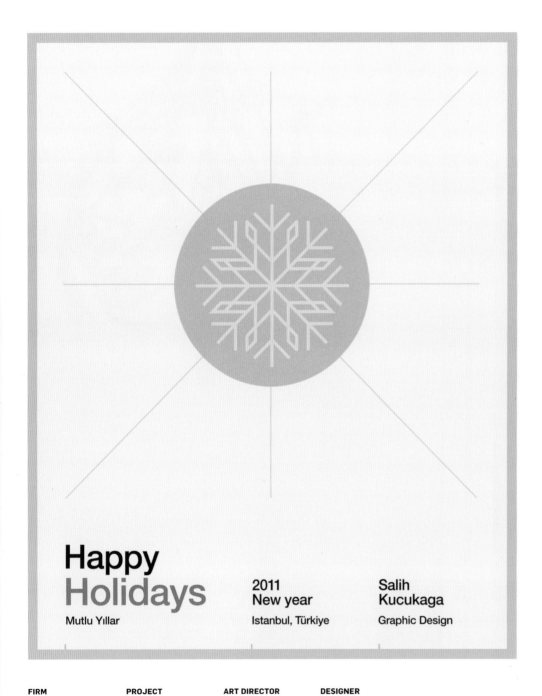

Happy
Holidays
Mutlu Yıllar

2011
New year
Istanbul, Türkiye

Salih
Kucukaga
Graphic Design

FIRM
Salih Kucukaga
Design Studio

PROJECT
2011–2012
New Year Card

ART DIRECTOR
Salih Kucukaga

DESIGNER
Salih Kucukaga

FIRM
Jeff Rogers

PROJECT
Christmas Card

DESIGNER
Jeff Rogers

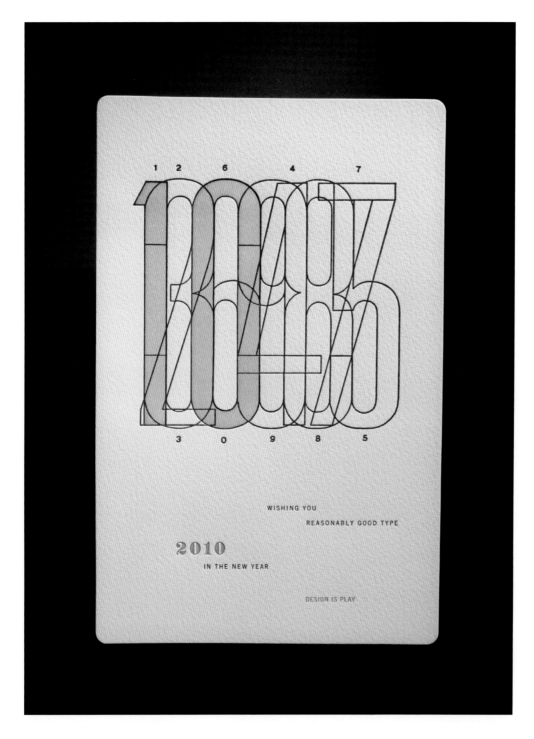

FIRM
Design Is Play

PROJECT
2010 New
Year Card

DESIGNERS
Mark Fox
Angie Wang

FIRM
SK Designworks

PROJECT
Season's Greetings
Holiday Promotion

ART DIRECTOR
Soonduk Krebs

DESIGNER
Soonduk Krebs

KATE BINGAMAN-BURT
Portland, Oregon

Physical or Digital?

I like to hold things in my hand. I like to look at things on my screen. When it comes to engaging with people about the things that I do, I've found a healthy balance by communicating sincerely online and then either zooming a special package off in the mail or giving surprise objects in person. Pro tip: everybody likes getting fun, unexpected mail.

My first website launched in 2002, and my first online store—filled with zines, drawings, and other small objects—launched on the same day. My work existed online as well as offline, and it has been that way ever since. I carried zines and buttons around rather than business cards. These objects were way more fun to hand out and to talk about than business cards and led to more meaningful discussions. They told good stories. I sent packages off to people not because I wanted a job, but because I simply liked what they made or the way they operated. These shipments would sometimes morph into a fun freelance project or other collaborations later down the road. Sometimes, they would just lead to a good friendship, which is just as valuable.

I try to convey this spirit to my students when the discussion of self-promotion or networking comes up. Here's what I tell them:

Have something to say. Don't just hand over a sweaty, generic business card and fail to make any eye contact to someone you have barely said two words to. Don't send a mass email out to tons of designers that you admire with a copy-and-paste form letter telling everyone how awesome you are as you ask for a job.

Take the time to research. Get to know the person you are reaching out to. Ask them questions rather than unloading your entire résumé in one long run-on sentence. Listen. Be sincerely interested in who you are speaking with.

Design a dang conversation piece. When my students embark on making their self-promos, I encourage them to create something that has a concept behind it and not something that just showcases their portfolio in miniature. If they are creating something tangible, I tell them to make something that people won't want to throw away, but will happily display on their desk or wall. If my students are emailing their website or PDF portfolio, I encourage them to drop off a handwritten note or specially made object in the mail to intended website viewers the same day. Leave a smart impression.

I don't want this to sound like an insincere formula. It's really tricky to navigate self-promotion in a personal and effective way. By combining research, multiple methods of communication, and a sincere interest in the people you are contacting, you will be off to an excellent start.

monoface

1

2

3

4

5

Five clickable areas:
Head & shoulders,
Right eye,
Left eye,
Nose,
and Mouth

Lighting and seamless
image editing handled
very well

759,375 possible
combinations of
features

monoface
happy new year from all of us.

monoface
happy new year from all of us.

back
1-10
759,375 faces
mono-1.com

FIRM	PROJECT	ART DIRECTOR	DESIGNER
mono, inc.	monoface	mono, inc.	mono, inc.

monoface

happy new year from all of us.

what do i do?
shuffle face
view gallery

mono-1.com

monoface

happy new year from all of us.

what do i do?
shuffle face
view gallery

mono-1.com

Clean, open layout
creates immersive
experience with
images.

FIRM
The Allotment

PROJECT
Website

ART DIRECTORS
James Backhurst
Michael Smith
Paula Talford

DESIGNER
James Backhurst

Good Fucking Design Advice.
Serving the working class designer since 2010.

Promote your fucking self.

This isn't enough, I need more fucking advice.

Buy Our Merchandise

Clients got you down? Looking for
motivation to continue on? Complete
your life with one of our products.

Take the GFDA Pledge

Take the pledge. Get shit done. Never
accept another's standard for success
ever again.

Try the Family Friendly Version of GFDA

In a very concerted effort to clean up
our act, we've resurrected the family
friendly version of our site.

Created by Brian Buirge + Jason Bacher.

© 2010–2012 GFDA
Inspired by this and this.

FIRM	PROJECT	ART DIRECTORS	DESIGNERS
Good Fucking Design Advice	Website	Jason Bacher Brian Buirge	Jason Bacher Brian Buirge

WHAT WE DO

Custom design is all about the right solution for the right project. And when it comes to your project, it's all about opening our eyes and ears. We love working with forward-thinking, passionate individuals with a burning desire to share their vision. If that sounds like you, then here's the good news — we have the enthusiasm, and experience, to make your project sing. Because in the world of graphic design, we've kept busy. Working with clients both small and large, we've developed brand identities, logos, websites, blogs, stationery, campaigns, custom illustrations, packages and seemingly everything in between. But why toot our own horns? Take a look around, we think you'll like what you see.

SAMPLES

TELLING YOUR WEDDING STORY

From New York to New Brunswick, Athens to Arizona, Calgary to California and everywhere in between, love has a story to tell. Whether you met in line at your favourite concert, through an 'accidental Like' on Facebook, or on a good old-fashioned blind date, the details are important. And we take the phrase 'It's all in the details' to a whole new level. Working with fine papers and a variety of printing methods, we produce one-of-a-kind pieces from your first save-the-date to your last wedding favour. We'll approach your wedding with unmatched enthusiasm, using our vintage charm, clever storytelling and an affection for the unexpected to ensure a lasting impression for you and your guests.

Head on over to our info/pricing page for more information!

OUR STORY

We are a pair of cards is what we are. Not the King and Queen though, more like the Joker and the Ace (you can guess which is which). Whether debating design, hunting for treasure, traveling the globe or planning our next move, our story is one filled with excitement and a thirst for adventure. Sifting through flea markets in Brooklyn, navigating the skies of Switzerland, sampling pubs in Germany and relaxing right here in the Prairies are just a few of the ways in which we gather ideas, and that's the way we like it.

With 14 years of collective knowledge in graphic design, and an eye for opportunity, we use our wide-cast experience to approach any and all projects. From retail to manufacturing, cosmetics to construction, weddings to fashion and a variety of other industries, we've seen it all. Well, almost.

We are One Plus One, and our passion for a good idea is one that burns bright. That's our story, now let us hear yours.

FIRM	PROJECT	ART DIRECTOR	DESIGNER
One + One Design	Website Design + Development	Tyler + Jessie Thiessen	Tyler + Jessie Thiessen

FIRM	PROJECT	ART DIRECTOR	DESIGNER
mono, inc.	Younicorn App	mono, inc.	mono, inc.

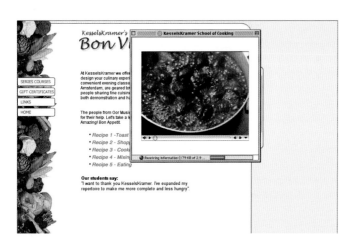

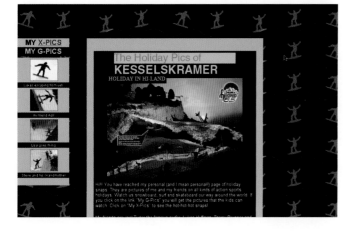

FIRM
KesselsKramer

PROJECT
Website

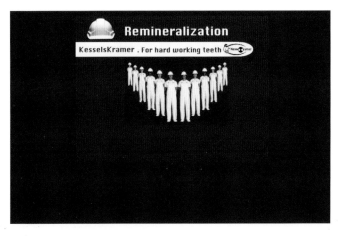

FIRM
Entermotion

PROJECT
Portfolio

ART DIRECTOR
Joe Marrow

DESIGNER
Joe Marrow

Main Menu

Contact

THE IDEA IS KING.

In the right hands, one idea can change the course of business. It can help a company redefine its destiny – turning breaking even into bursting at the seams. You see, all it takes is one great idea to take a brand from something it was, and turn it into everything it wants to be. Luckily for you, we have a lot of great ideas. **HELLO. WE'RE SHINE UNITED.**

◄ ► 1 2 3 4 5 6 7

SHINE PRESS
Shine Co-Founder and Executive Account Director Curt Hanke authors column for *Ad Age Magazine.* >>**READ MORE**

FEATURED WORK
Among our many Harley-Davidson projects, our work for The Harley-Davidson Museum is one of our favorites. >>**VIEW WORK**

SHINE NEWS
Shine United: The name change reflects the exploding digital world that includes websites and social media >>**VIEW NEWS**

Main Menu

Contact

SHINE NEWS

We Are Now Shine United.

Continued success plus more people plus expanded services equals a new name, a fresh logo and a bigger, shinier, space. >>**READ MORE**

◄ ► 1 2 3 4 5 6 7

SHINE PRESS
Shine Co-Founder and Executive Account Director Curt Hanke authors column for *Ad Age Magazine.* >>**READ MORE**

FEATURED WORK
Among our many Harley-Davidson projects, our work for The Harley-Davidson Museum is one of our favorites. >>**VIEW WORK**

SHINE NEWS
Shine United: The name change reflects the exploding digital world that includes websites and social media >>**VIEW NEWS**

FIRM
Shine United

PROJECT
Website

ART DIRECTOR
Michael Kriefski

DESIGNER
Jeff Szpak

FIRM
Willoughby Design

PROJECT
Willoughby
Holiday Card

ART DIRECTOR
Ann Willoughby

DESIGNER
Kevin Garrison

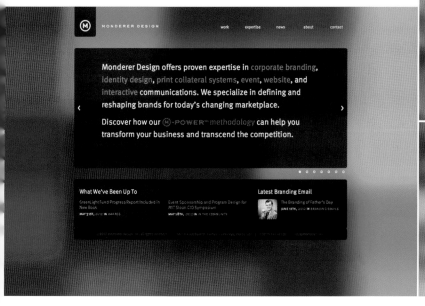

FIRM
Monderer Design

PROJECT
Website

ART DIRECTOR
Stewart Monderer

DESIGNER
Stuart McCoy

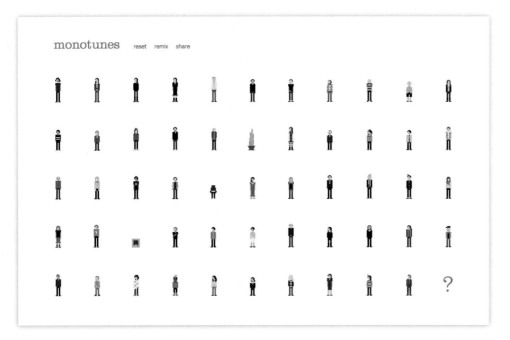

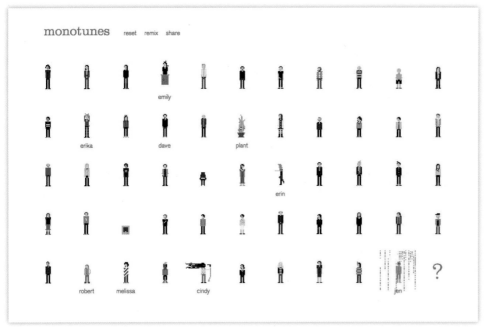

FIRM
mono, inc.

PROJECT
monotunes

ART DIRECTOR
mono, inc.

DESIGNER
mono, inc.

Getting Shit Done.

FIRM
Good Fucking
Design Advice

PROJECT
Video

ART DIRECTORS
Jason Bacher
Brian Buirge

DESIGNERS
Jason Bacher
Brian Buirge

ANDREW SHEA
New York, New York

Write, Designers, Write.

We write more than ever. Many of us spend several hours each day crafting emails. We fine-tune creative briefs and send scores of text messages. Our sketchbooks include lists, reminders, and the occasional epiphany. Yet few of us consider ourselves to be writers. In fact, most of the designers I talk to claim to be bad writers.

So where do timid writers start? Here are three suggestions:

First, recognize a key similarity between good writing and good design: it results from a process. This short passage involved research, brainstorming, a first draft, revising, a final draft, revising, and proofing. It is similar to most design projects that I start. I had no idea what the final product would be, but I trusted the process and each step revealed a new idea or detail until I finished it.

Next, designers can become more confident writers by telling the stories about their projects. For example, you might describe the different stages of a project: the design challenge, the research, your goals for the design, how you executed highlights of the design, and what your design achieved. This approach will make the writing process more enjoyable because it invites more of your voice, opinions, and personality.

Last, edit and refine the text until it clearly conveys what you want to communicate. I usually follow three simple edit tips: read the text out loud, listen to your computer read the text, and change the typeface of the text to something dramatically different every time you edit it. These tips should help you locate errors with ease and will likely inspire you to make important updates along the way.

Whether you need to write project descriptions for potential clients, essays about design, or cover letters for job applications, clear writing can distinguish inexperienced designers from experienced ones.

Base
Art Co.

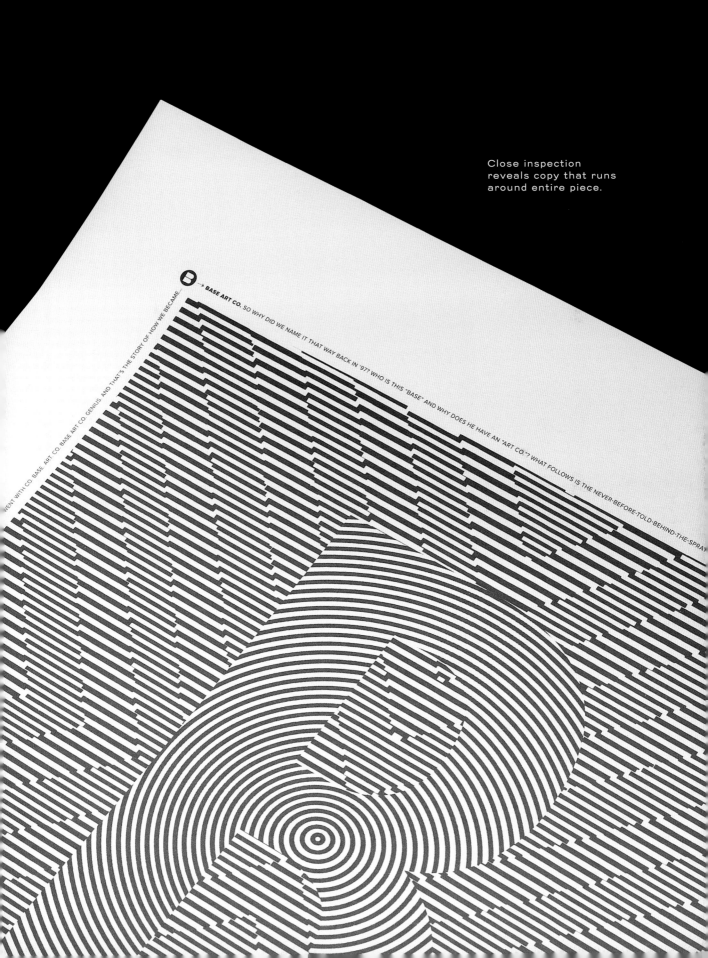

Close inspection
reveals copy that runs
around entire piece.

BASE ART CO. SO WHY DID WE NAME IT THAT WAY BACK IN '97? WHO IS THIS "BASE" AND WHY DOES HE HAVE AN "ART CO."? WHAT FOLLOWS IS THE NEVER-BEFORE-TOLD-BEHIND-THE-SPRAY

WENT WITH CO. BASE ART CO. BASE ART CO. GENIUS. AND THAT'S THE STORY OF HOW WE BECAME

Visually arresting with
competing patterns

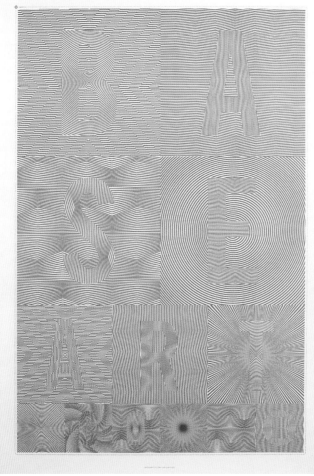

Varied visual
experiences when
comparing close
and far views

FIRM
Base Art Co.

PROJECT
"The Story of How"
Poster

ART DIRECTOR
Terry Rohrbach

DESIGNERS
Terry Rohrbach
Drue Dixon

CLOSER LOOK

Good Fucking Design Advice

Black on black printing creates a subversive feeling.

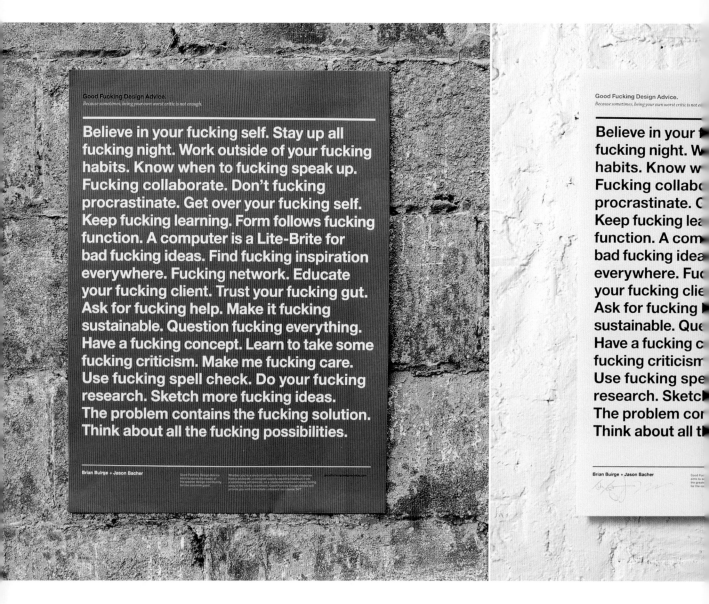

Neutral, sans serif
typography provides a
sense of calm among
hard-hitting copy.

FIRM	PROJECT	ART DIRECTORS	DESIGNERS
Good Fucking	Posters	Jason Bacher	Jason Bacher
Design Advice		Brian Buirge	Brian Buirge

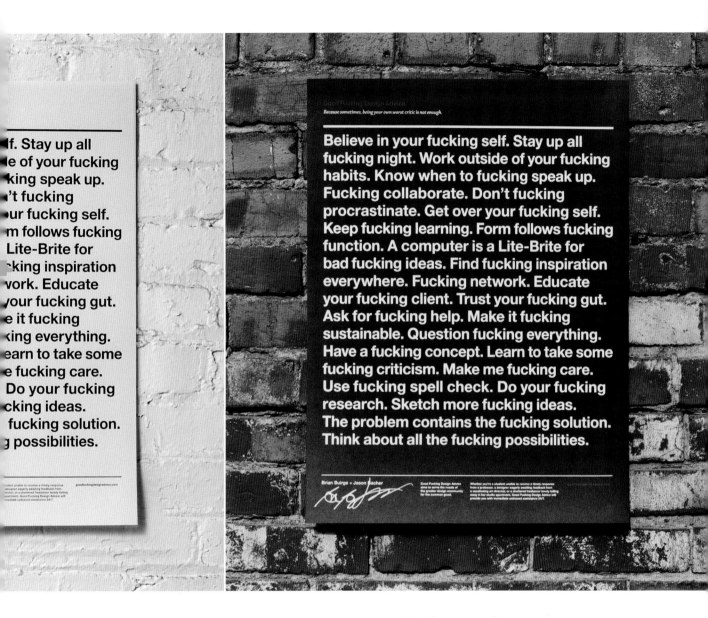

Raw language shot
on rough surfaces to
reinforce message

About the Author

Go Welsh is a design studio based in Lancaster, PA.

Its work has received recognition from the world's leading creative competitions (Cannes Lions, D&AD, One Show, One Show Design—Best of Show) and publications (*Communication Arts*, *Coupe*, *Graphis*, *How*, *Print*, and Rockport Publishers).

The studio's principal, Craig Welsh, serves as an assistant professor of communications and humanities at Penn State Harrisburg and teaches in the MFA graphic design program at Marywood University in Scranton, PA.

gowelsh.com

PROJECT
Custom Moleskine® Notebook Printed in
the Go Welsh Letterpress Print Shop

Dear Sir or Madam. Congressman. Jelly of the Month Club Member. John. Many Thanks. Cordially Yours. Our Warmest Wishes. Yours Truly. Best Regards. Sincerely. **Go Welsh.**

PROJECT
The Every-occasion Notecard

Craig Welsh
cwelsh@gowelsh.com

3055 Yellow Goose Road
Lancaster, PA 17601

tel 717 898 9000
fax 717 898 9010

www.gowelsh.com

Most people have good business cards. So do we. Loads of them. But we're not handing them out anymore because we're sick of good business cards. We want great business cards. That's why we're still working on them. We're not satisfied with 99% good enough business cards. So until they're done, all you get is this. But be assured, in the not too distant future, you're going to get a great business card. **Go Welsh**

Scott Marz
smarz@gowelsh.com

3055 Yellow Goose Road
Lancaster, PA 17601

tel 717 898 9000
fax 717 898 9010

www.gowelsh.com

No, I don't have a title. None of us do. Something about titles don't amount to much, it's a level playing field, we all do everything and aren't confined by what our business card says. Because one day I'm designing but the next day I could be asked to come up with a headline or direct a photo shoot or take out the garbage and this way I can't say "Whoa, hold on there. That's not what my business card says." **Go Welsh**

Corie Deshong
cdeshong@gowelsh.com

3055 Yellow Goose Road
Lancaster, PA 17601

tel 717 898 9000
fax 717 898 9010

www.gowelsh.com

We actually started with a business card design that was really interesting. Absolutely amazing colors. They were beautiful! Then we got the printing quotes. Ouch. Paper cut ouch. But we needed something. ANYTHING. Which is how we arrived at this sucker. I don't have anything against black. Or gray. Or white. My beef is with drab. I pray this card meets the shredder and the pretty ones are resurrected. **Go Welsh**

PROJECT
Personalized Business Cards Written by
Individual Staff Members

Contributors

Bill Simone: 1956 – 2012

Acknowledgments

Thanks to everyone who submitted work for this publication and those who were involved in its design: Scott Marz, Greg Bennett, Corie Deshong, and Pammi Simone. An additional nod to the wonderfully gifted essay writers: Nick Asbury, Doug Bartow, Kate Bingaman-Burt, Robynne Raye, and Andrew Shea.

A sincere expression of gratitude to Emily Potts, Regina Grenier, Cora Hawks, Winnie Prentiss and all the talented and helpful members of Rockport Publishers for your guidance and encouragement.

Lastly, heartfelt recognition of the thoughtful, inspired photography of Bill Simone. You helped fill many portfolios with beautiful, compelling images.